MW00719323

Reflections
of the Soul

Marie Sword, wife of author.

Reflections of the Soul

Gene Sword

VANTAGE PRESS
New York

FIRST EDITION

Copyright © 1999 by Gene Sword

Published by Vantage Press, Inc.
516 West 34th Street, New York, New York 10001

Manufactured in the United States of America
ISBN: 0-533-12891-9

Library of Congress Catalog Card No.: 98-90690

0 9 8 7 6 5 4 3 2 1

Contents

Foreword

Although this book is a collection of poems, its main purpose is to tell the reader about a profound love that existed between two people. A love that came into being at a precise moment in one of those lives, that prevented a tragic waste of life. It's the age old story. Boy meets girl. Boy gets girl. They live happily ever after. Not quite! This is a true story. Oh, it's true that boy met girl and boy got girl and they did live happily for twenty-three years. But then, the dreaded curse of mankind struck, through fate, and tore that love asunder. There is hardly a life today that has not been touched at least once by the cursed fiend called cancer. If it has not struck your life yet then you are blessed. But, my friend, the chances are great that it will strike your loved ones or even you in your lifetime. The story is not about cancer. It's about love and the joy of living.

I endeavored to make this book different than any book of poetry that I have ever seen. I tried to do that by combining prose and poetry into one book. Usually, people are "turned off" by poetry. I find this is true chiefly because the poetry is not "readable." This book is an effort to make each poem readable. A poem is nothing more than a short story that is told in verse form by a person who finds it easier to use verse than prose. If you do not now like poetry, I sincerely hope this approach will cause you to have a different slant and make you take a different tack about poetry in the future. It's a wonderful way to relax. If a poem does not relate to a story one can understand, what good is it and who will read it?

I shall never forget an incident while I was monitoring a poetry class in a well-known university that illustrates the point I am trying to make about "readable" poetry and what some folks do with poetry. I do not now recall the poet or the title of the poem. However, I recall the incident vividly. The professor had presented a poem about a snow scene that was dissected by an old rail fence. The poet told a beautiful tale and described the scene in verse magnificently, clearly and vividly. But as usual, some pseudo-intellectual thought he should point out the Freudian implications set forth by the poet. It was none of that. I was so disgusted with such maligning of a beautiful poem, I walked out of the class. It was obvious the poet was simply describing a beautiful scene in winter and was trying to impart that beauty to the reader's mind.

Let me reiterate by saying this book is a love story about two people who met, fell in love and lived life fully until one of them died from cancer. It is about the psychological pain, the physical pain and the grief felt by the survivor. It is about the exhilarating feelings of being in love and living that love to the fullest. It's about the heartbreak of parting, the coping when all your plans for the future come crashing down. It's about the "Angels" who helped before death, during and after, and there are many. It's true. It's my life and the life of my "Lady Rose." It is truly "The Reflections of the Soul." My soul.

Acknowledgments

This book is dedicated to the memory of my late and beloved wife Rose Marie, who inspired me to write, insisted I pursue the task and never let me rest when I tried to slack off. Without her I would never have published a single line. Her love lifted me up and saved me. Her watchful eye saw that I never again threw a scrap of paper away with a note or a poem on it. Her courage sustained me and made it possible for me to attend to her needs during her long suffering and death. Her candor, her confidence, and her encouragement prompted me to put my thoughts on paper. She inspired me and there is little doubt that she was the wind beneath my wings. This was a very special lady I speak about and my only regret is that the entire world did not know her. I can honestly say and I have heard the remark made by others also—"If you knew Marie, you could not help but like her." I thank her from the bottom of my heart and I am so glad this woman knew exactly how I felt about her while I could still speak and she could still hear. I shall always remember the words "I love you." They ring inside my mind like a hammer striking steel and they leave an indelible mark upon my soul that will never be eradicated, not even by time.

I thank Dr. Norman L. Dodge for being my mentor, for his friendship and his kind encouragement in this endeavor. His help was invaluable. I would like to thank my friends and neighbors for allowing me to use them as a sounding board. I especially want to thank Beverly Raulen for her expert help on the computer and desktop publishing. Bev was Marie's best friend and is still my friend and advisor. Her help was invaluable. My friend and neighbor Sally Virgil was my proofreader and sounding board. If it wasn't right with her, it was rewritten. Her help can't be measured. Thank you, Sally. I also thank Helen Burrow for her help and assistance and input.

My thanks also go out to my daughters Janine and Jamie who have provided help and encouragement. Janine assisted me in the area of copyrights and publishing, having herself had experience in the field of authorship and publishing. There are numerous people who gave useful suggestions and advice. I drew upon every source of help available to me. Most of all, I thank the "almighty one" who sustained my strength and resolve throughout this ordeal and guided my steps, sometimes unwillingly, down the narrow path that has brought me to this place in time.

This acknowledgment would not be complete without thanking Crown of Texas Hospice. Without these Angels of Mercy, Marie's last days would have been unbearable. Her assigned nurse, Eunice Jordan, is the most caring, dedicated, knowledgeable, efficient, and compassionate human being I have ever encountered. She prepared me for, and guided me through the most difficult period of my life on this earth. Mrs. Jordan has earned a place of veneration in my heart for as long as I live. With the most profound humility I can muster, I thank you Eunice. The Chaplain, Doug Fisk; and the home health aides, Sue Burleson and Annie Henderson, were also extremely helpful. When one sees a team so dedicated and proficient, the attention always turns to the "power behind the machine." In this case it has to be Marsha Irwin, Ph.D., RN, the director of Crown. Thank you Marsha. Dr. Irwin has put together a complete service program, consisting of immediate care, bereavement management, social activities, a volunteer program, luncheons and outings, that is most helpful in such a time of crisis.

Reflections
of the Soul

I

In the Beginning

Rose Marie Hughes was born on a cool, crisp, gusty morning. It was March 27, 1946, just after World War II. Truly a "baby boomer" in every sense, she took her first breath on a farm in Monette, Arkansas, among clean, loving, honest but meager surroundings. The first born to the union of Russell Hughes and Georgia Mask. Russell lost his first wife who left him with four children to raise alone. Georgia's first marriage ended in divorce and left her with one child to also raise alone. The Hughes–Mask marriage produced one more child, a boy. Now the situation consisted of "Mine," "Yours" and "Ours;" a prime condition for conflict. But, there was none of that. The Hughes family was well thought of in the small farming community of Monette and they grew and prospered within reason. The Hughes became a very close family and when one member was in distress they all rallied around the problem until it was solved. Truly a family of love.

As life always goes when the birds fly the nest, each grew up, finished school and in time moved away. And so it was with Rose, who came to be called by her middle name Marie. The promised land of California was the place to go in those days. The war had helped to glamorize Hollywood and it was touted as the "Land of Opportunity." Her heart knew what the wild goose knew. She went to California.

While in California she met her first husband who was in the armed forces at the time. After his discharge they moved back to

1

Arkansas and subsequently to Texas. The marriage ended after nine years, leaving her to live alone in a large city, with a bad taste for marriage but a healthy yearning for love. The kind of love a woman really dreams about but thinks she will never find, yet never stops looking for. A beautiful, vibrant woman, just twenty-eight years of age and marking time. She was not well schooled in the wicked ways of the world. Her former life had pretty much shielded her from that type of thing. Yet, she thirsted for knowledge and read constantly. She educated herself.

Gene came from a different world. An only child, born to an Appalachian coal miner in unimaginable poverty, his parents were good, respectable people with a history that dated back to the Pilgrims. However, the coal-mining slums forced him to fight his way to and from school almost daily. That kind of life made him hard and self-sufficient. He yearned for a good education and the opportunity to lift himself from the coal dust. To be somebody. To be respected. He vowed to himself to do just that. Such determination carried him to distant places and involved him in happenings he could not begin to imagine in those early days.

Gene tried college for a while, but without financial help from his poverty-stricken family, it was a "no win" situation as employment was hard to come by in Appalachia. He certainly wasn't going to be an iceman or truck driver all his life. The year was 1947, one year after Marie was born. Congress was considering creating a separate U. S. Air Force, and so they did. The Air Force was hungry for volunteers to build up the fledgling service. They made some attractive offers to prospects. It was right up Gene's alley. A chance to fly, see the world and get an education at the same time. "Boy am I going to make you a deal," type of thing.

Off he went "Into the wild blue yonder." First to basic training, which was still tough in those days. Out of basic, hard as nails and looking for challenges. Communications and electronics was the magic bubble back then and it was for him. Out of communications and electronics and into flying cadets. Then he went into

2

teaching. There, he foolishly married one of his students, after she graduated.

The whirlwind kept blowing! Wow! A full-blown war and away to Korea! By this time he was the father of two. In his next home, the mighty 20th Air Force, Gene was assigned to the 19th Bomb Wing, 28th Bomb Squadron, and made several hair-raising missions into MIG alley. While in Korea, his new wife was anything but "true." Soon he had five children.

Into the secret intelligence world he went, with school after school until he was sick of education. In his forties, disillusioned with life, his government and a miserable marriage, he easily agreed to a divorce when the opportunity presented itself.

He began his freedom vowing he would stay single for life. By now he was senior agent in charge of a local federal investigative agency, decorated by war and commended by superiors for a "job well done." He didn't *feel* "like a job well done." It was time to retire and find a new life. And so he did. With his investigative experience he was a "shoo-in" for an opening as an insurance investigator. A job that almost got him killed by organized crime when he stepped on their toes. Four of his five children were now college age—and the dollars wouldn't stretch. So, extra jobs where are you? He ended up with three in addition to his regular job as an insurance investigator for a large firm. One of those extra jobs was managing the largest supper club on the Gulf Coast at the time.

Divorced, alone and overworked, he went "middle aged crazy." He tried everything from skydiving to stock car racing. Nothing helped. Tired of booze, tired of fast cars, fast women, promiscuity, job dangers, adrenaline highs, bad memories and an ex-wife who would not let him be, he moved to Texas. There he went to work for a large grocery chain as a security agent. Marie just happened to work for the same company; he didn't meet her though, until fourteen months later.

Bad habits are hard to break. Gene lost his father in 1966 and

3

his mother in 1972. He moved to Texas the year his mother died. The loss cut a hole deep into the fabric of his soul. So back to the fast life he went. Night clubs and different women every night. His adopted brother now joined him and they made a carousing pair.

In mid-August 1973, Gene went shopping at a grocery store near his apartment. While in the store the sun was shining through a skylight at an acute angle, illuminating the freezer section of the store in uncanny brilliant sunlight. A young lady was retrieving an object from a shelf over the freezer and as she did so the sun shone on her beautiful auburn hair and highlighted her emerald-green eyes. There was no denying it, he was smitten! After all those years as a bachelor, he was still skittish, so he didn't pursue the matter. Then on August 29, 1973, he was called to one of the chain stores about a problem. Who do you think came out of the courtesy booth? Yes! It was she!

Being on friendly terms with the store manager Gene asked him who the young lady was. "That is Marie," the manager replied, "and she recently got her divorce. Come on, I'll introduce you. She is nice." With that Gene met Marie, his "Lady Rose." No more time spent in night clubs or womanizing. From that day forward there was never anyone else but Marie twenty-four hours a day, and they lived their lives as one. That brings us to the first poem. It is called "My Lady Rose" and it tells the story of how her love turned a wasted life into one of meaning and purpose. There were no more booze sessions, no more hurt and no more loneliness. All replaced by the burning desire to get ahead, succeed and make a home for "My Lady Rose."

My Lady Rose

She found me in a wretched pool of pity
When my life could go nowhere but down
All I knew was booze, fights and nightclubs
With fast and easy women in sleazy gowns

My days and nights all ran together
I was two steps from the gutter all the time
My soul was bleeding, parched and barren
And I thirsted every moment for "demon wine"

I woke up every morning with a new face
On the pillow that lay beside me on the bed
I hated every moment of my existence
And I often wished that I would be found dead

But there was a purpose to all my failings
Somewhere, somehow, someone would need my love
And that purpose was in the form of a lady
Surely God had sent this lady from above

She came into my life in rays of sunlight
And that moment in my memory forever froze
In an instant she swept away my sordid past life
My "angel of the morning"—"My Lady Rose."

The scene of Marie caught in the sunlight, which highlighted her hair and her eyes, was so captivating, it inspired the writing of "Yonder Smiling."

Yonder Smiling

I spied a young girl shopping
Many years ago
When by chance our eyes did meet
And love began to grow

A sunbeam gleamed on auburn hair
Of which a lock was seen
To brush against a flawless cheek
Over eyes of emerald green

The moment was forever frozen
And lingers deep inside my mind
The scene will prod me ever onward
Like speeding sands of passing time

When one of us must travel on
The other to remain
I know if I must linger here
My heart will break with pain.

This wonderful, kind and loving lady deterred Gene from a wayward life, fraught with trouble, into one that could now foster dreams. A life of hope and prosperity, filled with loving moments of tenderness and passion. A life never known by Gene before and with a goodly chance he would never know again. Their love grew from moment to moment. Their courtship and engagement lasted for two years. Finally on March 29, 1975, they became husband and wife. His "Lady of the Morning;" his "Lady Rose," with her effervescent personality and an enigmatic air about her, inspired and encouraged him to express himself in the form of poetry. The following poems are a collection depicting that courtship and the early days of the marriage.

Take the Time to Dream

Take the time to dream awhile
Before each day begins
Feed the soul with "'manna"
When labors come to end

Remember everything on earth
Begins with someone's dream
And has a new beginning
When we take the time to dream.

Gene could now dream. He could plan. He was whole again. Every passing day drew him closer to being cleansed of the past hurts. Each new morning brought hopes everlasting and filled him with an exuberance that he could not explain. Every spare moment was spent in writing, correcting and rewriting poems expressing how he felt about life.

He saw beauty and meaning in obscure things such as a frog or snake in a pond. A grotesque, misshapen tree. A white-tailed buck deer with its breath forming puffs of white and rising condensation. All were subjects of beauty to him. A lowly scrap of driftwood held magical beauty for him. So he wrote while she encouraged. Gene had always expressed his inner feelings in poetry. The dark and brooding days of his life had given birth to dark and brooding poems, but happiness caused light and happy poems.

Wedding Day

In veil and gown of living pink
Is what my eyes did see
When first I saw her in the aisle
My loving bride to be

Every head inside the church
Turned and gave a smile
My bride to be drew ever near
To join me for awhile

The points of light within her eyes
Were shimmering emerald wells
That spoke of love she had to give
No human voice could tell

She lifted up her tender lips
When she received the ring
And as my arms engulfed her form
I heard an angel sing

If I should live a hundred years
And travel down life's way
With my last thought I'll think out loud
"I'll never forget that day."

Bluebonnets

Bluebonnets bloom in the spring of the year
They seem to cover the land
Paintbrush hide among the blooms
As only paintbrush can

Green is the grass in the fields where they grow
Accenting these delicate flowers
Bewitching all who chance to see
This colorful blossom shower

I recall a young girl sitting there
On a knoll kissed by the sun
That maiden stole my heart away
We lived our lives as one

We returned to the knoll beside the road
Whenever we wished to feel free
While sitting there among the flowers
I held the hand of Marie.

Wild Geese

The morning was crisp with "Jack Frost"
'Neath skies of azure blue
Made breath hang in white puffs
As dawn came breaking through

We watched the rice fields westward
Where wild geese often flew
And saw the flocks descending
Onto stubble and the dew

The morning smells delighted us
Our hearts beat as one
As we realized our depths of love
In the first rays of the sun

The rice fields are all gone now
Replaced by urban "shove"
But every time I pass the place
I'm reminded of her love.

Waste Not One Moment

Let me hold you while I may
Before tomorrow comes
And robs us of the time we have
That passes with each sun
We'll take each day as they arrive
Each moment as we can
We'll savor chances we contrive
To hold each other's hand

I'll kiss your lips; I'll touch your cheek
And brush away each tear
Recalling all the happiness
In every passing year
Not a second wasted
For each is gone for good
Let memories be of pleasant things
Like love, as well we should.

II

True Love Grows

True love really does grow. So it was with Gene and Marie. They made many friends, prospered and were happy. In 1978 they bought their first home in a new subdivision near Lake Side Airport, in Houston, Texas, from which Gene flew small planes as a hobby. By now they were inseparable. Gene started a security business of his own and Marie resigned her job as booth supervisor for the large grocery chain. She began managing Gene's office for him as his duties took him afield quite often. Marie was always there for Gene in all of his endeavors, even when he went back to college at Texas A&M for graduate work. When school or business kept them apart they called each other two or three times daily. It was pure agony for both of them when they were not together. Most will tell you a couple cannot get along if they work together, go home together and go out together. Those two did, and loved every moment of it. Either would gladly have died for the other without question.

As their days together became golden, they built a bond so strong it was not understood by outsiders. They were so close they knew what the other was thinking and what the other one was going to say, before any words were spoken. Often an answer was given by the other to an unspoken question. They amazed themselves at times. There was no explaining such a love. If one hurt, the other hurt also. If one was upset or cried, so did the other. There was never a moment of distrust or doubt. Each knew without question the other would be faithful no matter how strong the temptation. It went without saying. Each always knew where the other one was and come dark, they were always home together.

Gene worshiped "his lady." Sometimes he awoke in the morning and would just lie beside her, watching her sleep. Soon, she would stir from slumber and instinctively reach out her arms to him. They would lie there, he in her arms and she in his, each not wanting to let go. Thus they would stay for long periods of time. After selling their home and moving to the country they practiced this ritual and would lie silently, listening to the many songbirds and their different songs. They were so in love and delighted with life. The following poems are meant to show that.

Beware the Rose

In all of God's creation
The rose is best by far
With perfect leaf and petal
Reaching toward a star

They nod their heads in sunlight
While dancing on a breeze
And waft their sultry fragrance
Our senses they do tease

They are the queen of all flowers
And jealous I am told
If you plant a flower next to one
No blossom will unfold

Beware and do not pick one
For you will feel distress
The flower is armed with thorns you see
That will surely tear your flesh.

Wine and Roses

In the days of "Wine and Roses"
When our love was flowing free
Between two hearts so faithful
As deep in love as love could be

We danced to songs that made us happy
We vowed we would forever be
Two hearts as one would beat forever
For all the world and God to see

Through happy days, strife and trouble
We walked through life hand in hand
We weathered grief and tribulation
We went through hell and back again

The fire of love burned bright and smoldered
Through days, weeks, months and years
"The bond of love" binds hearts eternal
Undaunted by life's grief and tears

All our days were "Wine and Roses"
We smelled the flower; we drank the wine
We prayed to God it would last forever
You gave me your heart. I gave you mine.

Sit with Me a Moment

Sit with me a moment
Before the night begins
Let's share our love in private
And dream our dreams again

We'll speak of all the places
That we would like to go
We'll talk about our garden
And the seeds that we should sow

I'll whisper tender love words
Softly in your ear
And vow my love forever
Which only you shall hear

I'll hold your hand so gently
You'll hardly feel my touch
Our hearts will speak in unison
"I love you very much."

Dance with Me

Come dance with me my love
Let's while the night away
We'll let the magic music
Sound 'til the break of day

Your gown will catch the breeze
As we whirl about the floor
My arms will form a circle
And enclose you ever more

The world outside forgotten
As our journey we prepare
We will drift away together
And boldly we will dare

We'll drink enchanted potions
That set the mind afar
We'll don bewitching slippers
And tiptoe through the stars

We'll catch a glowing moonbeam
For all the world to see
The cup of life sustains us
We will in love forever be.

Recalling Springtime

I recall the breath of springtime
When grass was green and lush
We'd sit together basking
In the silence and the hush

The nearness of your presence
Made my poor pulse rush
Then I'd steal a kiss from you
Which caused your cheeks to blush

The songbirds in the forest
Sang their sweet refrain
The trees were tall and shading
And were of many strains

The flowers were bright with color
Washed and nursed by rain
Love was sweet in springtime
Like the love songs that we sang.

III

Write for Me

They were growing older, and as much in love as they had been in those early days when the blood ran hot in their veins. They could hardly wait to be alone in those private, intimate moments. While they were growing older, so did Marie's parents. On their many visits to Arkansas to see her parents, they both noticed how frail her father was becoming. Her mother was now in bed, most of the time. Georgia Hughes had suffered from a stroke and heart trouble which had been brought on by diabetes. Russell now had diabetes also. He exhibited some symptoms of dementia and it was apparent he was having difficulty with blood flow to his brain.

In 1988, Russell suffered a moderate stroke and entered the hospital. The doctors, in their physical examination of him, discovered a tumor in the opening of his bladder. A test was conducted, the tumor proved malignant. Surgeons removed the tumor and injected chemicals directly into the bladder. The treatment caused excruciating pain that resulted in extremely elevated blood pressure. The elevated blood pressure caused a massive stroke and Russell was never again able to speak or use one side of his body. His carotid arteries were almost totally blocked. Some months later he died.

Gene was semiretired at the time. Marie had taken a position as office manager with an importer of Danish furniture. Gene had received news of Russell's passing and was waiting to break the sad news to Marie. He knew she would need all the support he could give her and he was ready. When she arrived home from work, Gene held her and gently told her the bad news. She was distraught and heartbroken. Marie loved her father and his passing was a severe blow to her but Gene's strength carried her through.

They had taken some wild rides to Arkansas during Russell's illness. Especially when it appeared he was near death. On one occasion they had driven straight through the 500-mile journey at a sustained speed of ninety-five miles per hour. As strange as it seems, they were never stopped or given a ticket. This time, they drove sensibly. No need to rush now, it was over.

During the ordeal of the funeral, Gene never left Marie's side. He slept and ate only when she slept or ate. He held her for long hours at night, while she sobbed with grief and he hurt for her as much as she hurt for her father. Both tried to look after Georgia, whose health was also frail; the loss of Russell plainly took its toll on her. All of this was painful for Gene because he had come to love Marie's parents as much as he loved his own parents. Why not? They had accepted him and treated him as a son. There had never been the typical in-law syndrome in their relationship. Gene loved them so much he had bought a home in Monette for them, which Georgia and Russell had appreciated and enjoyed.

They stayed with Georgia for a while and then returned home to Texas. Marie went back to work and buried herself in her duties while Gene doted over her. She loved it. It helped her cope with her loss. Gene was writing some and working part-time at his business. But new government regulations had taken a toll on that business and it wasn't as demanding as it had been. (Of course, he wasn't making the money he had before the changes, either.)

The itch to leave the city and move north to the lake was infecting Gene daily. He spent time at the lake looking at real estate. Soon he talked Marie into joining him in his search for "Camelot." Finally, they were at the lake almost every weekend looking at houses and property. Nothing looked promising. Just as they were about to give up, they stumbled onto a rather large, two-story home, overlooking the lake on three sides. They both instantly knew this was their Camelot. When negotiations ended, they were owners of the house overlooking Pinwah Slough, on the wide part of the lake. They set about remodeling the house. Finally, Gene moved up to the lake; but Marie didn't move full-time until the following July. That arrangement didn't keep them apart though. Gene was in Houston one night and Marie was in Livingston the next. You couldn't keep those two separated long.

In July 1989, they moved to the lake full-time and Marie commuted to Houston daily for a time. Gene eventually talked her into retiring and living at the lake full-time. He worried about her commuting so far daily. There were so many "sickos" in the world in those days.

They fished, lay in the sun, gardened and grew flowers. When the opportunity presented itself, which was quite often, they visited her mother in Arkansas. They were ecstatically happy and enjoyed their home immensely.

A few years after moving to their new home in the country, the economy really went sour and interest rates dropped dramatically. Since Gene's retirement fund was interest sensitive, they lost a large amount of income. Never one to be outdone, Gene simply looked around for a common need in the area, knowing opportunity is based on a "need." Just as he knew it would be there, he found it. The affluent absentee home owner at the lake needed landscape work. Not afraid of hard work, Gene started his own business again, specializing in small construction and landscape. He did well and Gene and Marie were able to maintain their lifestyle.

The work was hard and Gene was getting older. He had developed diabetes but was controlling it quite well, thanks to all of his physical activity. Nevertheless, in 1994 he suffered a heart attack. Five months later, he suffered another. Marie was there for him through both operations. He did well but could not continue the hard physical work so he gave his business away to a friend.

Not one to give up, he went to insurance school, passed the state exam and began selling insurance. He did well at his new endeavor.

The years marched on and Georgia was failing fast. She pined her life away for Russell and was anxious, it seemed, to join him. Gene talked to her on the phone quite often. On one occasion, she was telling him about an episode she experienced when her heart started racing and she was gasping for breath while walking for a short distance. Gene tried to influence her to call an ambulance, but she would not. He knew what to do. He called her son, Leon, who lived nearby. It didn't take Leon long to get her to the hospital. It was a case of "You go now or I will physically carry you" type of thing, so she went. Sure enough, she had occluded cardiac arteries and would have to undergo open-heart surgery.

The entire family, as usual, gathered around her. On Thanksgiving Day of 1995, Georgia underwent open-heart surgery. She died in the recovery room. The family was devastated, needless to say. To this day Thanksgiving seems to have a blight on it.

Gene and Marie stayed even closer to each other from then on. She encouraged him to write often and read every word. She seemed to thirst for the poems. At Marie's insistence he submitted some to a publisher who liked them. Gene had actually been writing often since 1992. Marie liked two of the poems in particular and suggested he submit those for consideration. Both were published. Years earlier a few others had been published but his interest in poetry wasn't as acute then.

The loss of Marie's mother inspired the poem "Gone to God," which next appears. Georgia (Mom) was a brave woman. She didn't seem to fear dying at all. In fact, she seemed to look forward to it. Russell was gone as was most of her family. She talked to Gene a lot as they were very fond of each other. She stated if

God wanted her to stay on earth, she was ready; if He wanted to take her, she was also ready for that. She felt she knew more people and loved ones who had passed on than those she knew who were still alive. With those thoughts, here is "Gone to God."

Gone to God

With trembling hand she touched my brow
Reassuringly she did say
"Do not worry, I am ready
To leave this world or gladly stay
There are so many gone before me
I long to see some happy day"
A tranquil smile caressed her pale lips
As I slowly stepped away

Too soon came the beckon somber
As we gathered by her side
They had done all they could do
As we watched life's ebbing tide
Nevermore her pale hands trembled
They rested quietly by her side
The voice we loved now was silent
Gone to God with gentle sigh.

Gene now threw himself into writing poetry, which seemed to flow easily from his pen. When he was quiet and thoughtful, Marie had a way of pulling the verses from him, like a magnet. The following two poems have previously been published and appear in the anthologies *Dances on the Horizon* and *Best Poems of 1995*. Here are the poems "Driftwood" and "Death of Summer."

Driftwood

Driftwood floating on the water
Tossed by tide, wind and sand
Restless waifs of the forest
Doomed to wander distant lands
Some will drift along forever
Victims of the tempest breath
While others rest on lonely beaches
Awaiting time's rigid test
Crumbling, cracking, bleaching, breaking
Gone forever in the night
Some become the jealous treasure
Of some frugal searcher's sight

Ghostly shapes in silver moonlight
Eerie songs sung by wind
Cold and cutting callous feelings
Like the broken souls of men
Like a million shapeless teardrops
Cried for dreams that won't come true
Scattered over countless beaches
Changing shapes in day's first hue
Then some caring hand caresses
A gnarled shape in the night
While the relic of abandonment
Becomes a work of sheer delight.

Death of Summer

Oh fall, you tinted leaves of autumn
Tinged and hued by nature's hand
Emissaries of pending winter
Clothing hills and dunes of sand

Parasols, spinning wildly
From the lofty branch on high
Of the towering tree so noble
Reaching upward to the sky

Brisk and tingling breezes blowing
Showering colors across the land
Painting figures in autumn foliage
Winter's breath is close at hand

Soon the trees will be denuded
Stark and barren tall they stand
Creaking, moaning, bowing, swaying
As if to say they understand.

Once smitten by a wee bit of success, Marie was now going through old poems, sorting out and selecting what appealed to her. "Work on these," she would chide and work on them Gene did. Here are a few she liked.

Look Homeward

Golden dreams and sunbeams gleaming
Entwined together on the sand
Beside a living emerald ocean
On mystic shores of distant lands

Across the far-off broad horizon
Beneath the pristine sky of blue
Through the steaming teeming jungles
Exotic birds of every hue

Wild orchids' fragrant perfume wafting
On gentle cooling tropic breeze
That intoxicate and tease the senses
Nature's grand intent to please

Sweet nostalgic thoughts cascading
Enraptured notes of sweet refrain
Loudly call us ever onward
'Til at last we're home again.

Happy Seashells

Eternal tides are ever washing
Across the beach of silver sand
Stranding scores of happy seashells
A treasure for some searching hand
That comes down to water searching
For nature's bounty of contraband

Varied shapes of many sizes
Colors come in many hues
Some are found as single seashells
Others come by "threes and twos"
There to grace a searcher's basket
Or maybe turn a walker's shoe.

The Whisper Tree

Soft whispers sing a night song
As boughs begin to sway
The treetops start to undulate
In moonlight bright as day
Strong breezes briskly blowing
Wild dancers moan with glee
Enchanted chorus quietly singing
Songs of the cryptic whisper tree

Bright stars are drifting slowly
Across a silent midnight sky
Seem to weave a strange sad story
Of trees that gently sigh
They wail a song of eerie sadness
Forgotten dreams that won't come true
The whisper tree sings songs eternal
That ring forever sad and blue.

Observations

Red, green, brown, and gold
Against a cobalt sky
Are forest, hills, and humble bush
Near waterfalls on high
Cascading down moss-covered rocks
On rushing rivulets sly
Near boulders gray that line the bay
Where silver beaches lie

Yellow, red, white, and blue
On rolling fields of green
Are flowers, twigs, and humble weed
Where butterflies do teem

Flitting here and flitting there
As far as field is seen
Adjacent to the silver beach
Where jewels in sunlight gleam.

The Lawyer Tree

It stood there on the hillside
A strange and twisted shape
At odds with all the other trees
Far above the lake

Its trunk is gnarled and twisted
A grotesque ugly shape
Defying laws of gravity
As twisted as a snake

Reminding all who view it
The tree's as crooked as can be
This odd misfit of nature
The "crooked lawyer" tree

Even nature couldn't stand it
When Mother Nature sighed
The tree caught a virus
It wilted and it died.

Ghostly Image

A giant tree tall and wide
Stripped of twig, bud, and leaf
Eerie branches spreading down
Like ghostly tears of grief

The ruling monarch of the woods
Stands above what it commands
It reaches forth and touches all
With shapeless gnarled hands

A ghostly image to be sure
Too proud to sway or bend
It's lived thus a hundred years
Through drought, flood and wind.

Rainy Days

Dark gray rain clouds floating, drifting
Hug the treetops in faded light
Soaking chilling all beneath them
Muddying roads and fields alike

Towering storm clouds rushing climbing
Fill the sky like giant blight
Soaking all of nature's creatures
Crashing thunder and lightning bright

Do not despair, complain, or grumble
All will pass to one's delight
Blue skies coming surely swiftly
Bathing all in bright sunlight.

Where Does the Night Wind Go?

Dawn has broken when the sun comes up
And brings the day at last
But where does the weary night wind go
To ponder its distant past?
If I only knew that sacred spot
That secret quiet retreat
Where it hides by day to repair its soul
And dream in grateful sleep
If that I knew perhaps I too
Could wander about the land
Absorbing all that life could give
Time and time again.

Call of the Wild

The moon is full and the night is still
The wind is icy cold
A piercing cry from the hills above
Echoes haunting days of old
Mournful notes of the wild wolf's howl
Come coursing back brave and bold

Frost crystals form on the rocky ledge
The notes are heard for miles
Cold piercing eyes from shadows peer
At the valley for awhile
With lifted head and nostrils flared
The wolf will sing the call of the wild.

Highland Home

I see you rise majestically
Against a midnight sky
Cloaked in mist and wonderment
As you're ever growing nigh
After years of wanderlust
With empty days and nights
I'll once again know the love
I feel for you tonight

I'll stand upon your lofty peaks
And watch the eagle fly
I'll feel the wind and hear its song
In trees that touch the sky
Once more I'll pause upon a spot
Of ancient hallowed ground
And say hello to mom and dad
Before I travel down

I'll gaze upon your ageless slopes
And cliffs that moan and sigh
I'll watch the rays of morning sun
Bid the day arise
I know the time will come once more
For me to say "good-bye"
I'll smile and try to be so brave
But secretly I'll cry.

The Sound of Silence

When the night steals across the land
Robbing everything of light
And dark fingers stab the day
Like some creeping killing blight
Messengers across the ages
Telling tales of lost delight
Is this then the sound of silence
That comes again with pending night?

When darkness comes bleak with blackness
Rich with sounds that creatures sing
With specks of light that dart and flicker
Sights of night the firefly brings
Messengers across the ages
Telling tales of wondrous things
Is this then the sound of silence
That comes again with birth of spring?

Reflections of the Soul

Be not ashamed to say "I love you"
Or afraid to say "I care"
Give your heart away completely
Make those around you well aware
Freely give your hand in friendship
Let not hatred tarry there
We are what the world perceives us
Leave not your soul bleeding bare
When your brother sorely needs you
Do not wait to lend a hand
Love and kindness be not ashamed of
They are the attributes of man
When you help a child in trouble
And you guide them "over the sand"
The Creator sees and loves you kindly
He holds your future in His hand

Don't be too proud to say "I'm sorry"
When your words have been unkind
Don't hesitate to beg forgiveness
When it's plain you've acted blind
Let not anger dwell within you
For it grows and it's a sign
All the hurt you cause to others
Will return to you in kind

When tribulations are all around you
And you know not where to turn
Let your candle shine forever
Hold it high and let it burn
Be not afraid to share your sorrow
Or cry a tear in its turn
What you've given to your brother
A "Loving Master" will return
When your final race is over
And you cannot lift a hand
When your weary steps have ended
Across a rocky, stormy land
When you stand at last in judgment
With retribution close at hand
Be contrite when you utter
"I am but a mortal man."

A Voice from Far Within

A voice from far within ourselves
Sings a sad and mournful song
That tells a story rich in lore
Of broken promises far too long
A voice that speaks of broken dreams
And the deeds that were all wrong
The voice from far within ourselves
Still sings a sad and lonely song

A voice from far within ourselves
Tells of all we should have won
It speaks of things that might have been
And of the songs we left unsung
A voice that cries a lonely wail
About the tasks that were not done
This voice from far within ourselves
Speaks of days that will not come

A voice from far within ourselves
Bemoaning all that has been lost
Throughout the life that has been lived
From summer's heat through winter's frost
A voice that grudgingly condemns
The emptiness and wasteful cost
The voice from far within ourselves
Reminding us of all we've lost.

Floral Bouquet

These roses are alive today
Tomorrow they may die
Where the flower petals fall
Let the petals lie
Each one is a heartache
Each petal is a tear
That you have cried and suffered with
Through life's succeeding years
They fall to ground like snowflakes
And gather on the sand
You will know your love has found you
When they reach to take your hand.

The Noble Rose

Have you not seen the noble flower
With triple petals bold
In red, white, pink, and blue
And even blazing gold?
Its foliage green on prickly briar
And steeped in history books of old
The fragrant breeze that touched its bloom
Will travel miles untold

The dew will wash its face by morn
The sun will kiss its vine
On trellis tree and limb alike
Its presence will entwine
The bushes grow in patterned lines
In neat and modern rows
This gift that God has given us
The lovely noble rose.

Refill the Vessel

If one is empty as a vessel
Drained of nectar from within
And silent as a song yet sung
They are like sadness that never ends

The human soul was made to marvel
And love throughout its mortal life
Without such food the heart would wither
And be as night without a light

The snowbird wings its way to warm skies
Each time the winter's cold breath blows
The love-starved heart will cling to warm words
Just the way the snowbird knows

Be not afraid to voice your feelings
Or put your love into words
Refill the cup with sweetest nectar
Then count the words of love you heard.

The Coming of Camelot

Somewhere over the rainbow glowing
High above the starlit sky
Camelot awaits my coming
Where no more my soul will sigh
There will be no fields of honor
No more cause for hue and cry
At last to rest on green fields yonder
Amid the amity there on high

Hell it was what was endured
On fields of fire far below
The inner me with scorched soul burning
For solutions longed to know
To that end came I not willing
Simply thrust there like white on snow
The chariot that travels homeward
Carries this battered hulk too slow.

IV

Many Endeavors

Poets, song writers and philosophers are credited with the statement, "Love is better the second time around." That old saying was an absolute fact with Gene and Marie. They never tired of each other's bodies and they never tired of each other's minds. They would often spend hours caressing and exploring their bodies. Their lingering kisses lit a passion that only long sessions of lovemaking could satisfy. Gene could never forget the damp tenderness of her lips or the sweetness that lingered on his mouth long after the kiss was gone. He was haunted by the glowing warmth of her body lying next to him or the emptiness he felt when she slipped away in the night because she could not sleep. Often he would be up and beside her on those occasions to see what he could do to help with the problem. Sometimes she simply needed to be held and reassured and would fall asleep in his arms. Loving Marie was easier than anything he had ever done in his life and certainly was the most enjoyable. How a love such as theirs came to be or how it managed to grow daily was a mystery to both of them. They both knew that if either lost the other their very survival would be questionable.

They both existed just to exist for the other. Their cleanliness was immaculate and they were in fear that the least inattention to hygiene might offend the other. Neither would permit that. They were never too tired for the other's amorous advances, no matter how tired they might actually be. Somehow, the touch of the other seemed to revitalize the weary body and they vigorously pursued the intent of the other. How can such love be? Only God could tell the reason or the method and He seems to guard that secret well.

Marie was born on the 27th of the month and they were married on the 29th of that month. Gene was born the first of the following month. That made their birthdays and anniversary just two days apart. It was a custom to celebrate all three occasions with one big celebration. Gene fondly recalls one such special time. Marie took a long soaking bath, went to the beauty shop and donned her favorite gown. Gene prepared also. Marie carefully put on makeup and applied Gene's favorite perfume. They dined out and had a few quick dances. When the evening out had ended they were both anxious to proceed homeward with haste. Arriving at their home, they were both giggling like teenage children. Their hands were all over each other. Clothes began to fall in a trail toward the bedroom. By the time they arrived at bedside, there was nothing left to imagine because there were no clothes left. The champagne bubbles they had consumed at mealtime were coursing through their blood. Marie drew close against Gene. He took her in his arms while their lips found each other in the darkness. An electrifying energy flowed between them as they became aware of their hot, wet burning kisses and the damp heat of their bodies pressed together. Gene felt her body tremble as they gently sank onto their bed. It was as exciting and mysterious as their first time, even though they had been married for quite a while. Quite some time had passed when they emerged from their love bed, exhausted and completely satisfied. They spoke in unison, "Happy birthday and happy anniversary, darling." So it was in their love and they hoped it would be forever.

They encouraged each other in whatever endeavor fate took the other into. There was never any jealousy of the other's achievements. In fact, the complete opposite was true. Wherever they went, they went together and they left together. Whatever they did they did together. There was no such thing as man's work or woman's work for those two. They both helped each other in whatever the task might be. There was no "couch potato" syndrome for them either. It was not a case of the woman waiting on the man or the man henpecked by the woman. Their love consisted of a mutual respect in all things, personal, private and public.

Marie loved to read and Gene never infringed upon those private moments or interrupted in any way. Gene loved music and poetry. Marie always found or made time to listen to his music and to read his poetry. She constantly encouraged him to write, write and write. She never felt left out or neglected. Why should she? She was part of everything in his life and he in hers. With those thoughts the following selection of Gene's poems was chosen by Marie as promising creations and will cover the categories of novelty, religious, holiday, friends and patriotic. It is sincerely hoped the reader likes them as much as Gene enjoyed creating them and sharing them with you. Marie enjoyed them and felt that others might also enjoy.

Novelty Poems

The Weary Outlaw

From a distance come sounds of hoofbeats
On the hot and hard-parched ground
Little dust puffs rising, drifting
Towards the sagebrush all around
Out of the sunset drifts a rider
Tall and slender, tanned, and brown
Wearing buckskins with silver spangles
With his brown hat of low-slung crown

The lonely horseman is slowly plodding
Ever eastward in fading light
At last he pauses on the prairie
Searching back trails in fading light
Then he quickly dismounts the saddle
He eats cold beans by dim starlight
His night bed's hard, cold, and rocky
With leather pillow and blankets light

As the pre-dawn hour approaches
A figure stirs from fitful sleep
And mounts the horse without his coffee
The outlaw rides in ground fog deep
He shifts the six-gun in its holster
He senses trouble as the trail grows steep
A single gunshot shatters silence
The outlaw rests at last in sleep.

The Eagle

From lofty heights in crystal skies
Above the crags that moan and sigh
In icy winds that numb the eyes
A single eagle turns and dives

Far below in seas of grass
A frightened hare rests at last
He stares across the plains so vast
As fatal talons close in fast

The hunter's folded wings unfurl
Its body flares as claws uncurl
The hare is snatched from hidden worlds
Rushing winds the dust does swirl

A feeble cry . . . then labored flight
The eagle climbs with all its might
To hidden nest far out of sight
And feeds its young before the night

Once more the rapture is on the wing
With joyful heart it starts to sing
The piercing notes from hillsides ring
As the eagle hunts for living things.

The Frog and Snake

There he sits on a lilypad
Singing a song of glee
King of the pond and cattail patch
Foretelling all he's free

He's green, black, and slimy, too
And he leaps from pad to pad
He's making eyes at Mrs. Frog
But she is cross and sad

He captures bugs with sticky tongue
And offers them to her
Mrs. Frog sits and stares
And never even stirs

The King doesn't see that big black snake
That's looking awfully grim
He disappears in the black snake's mouth
And that's the end of him

Now she is Queen of the lilypad
And a smile is on her face
She blinks her eyes and darts her tongue
At a bug with wings of lace.

Religious Poems

I Had a Talk with God Today

I had a talk with God today
Somehow I know He heard
I didn't ask for things myself
And God spoke not a word

I prayed He'd linger near you
As you begin each day
To shower your soul with blessings
And to walk with you a way

I asked that He grant you happiness
In everything you do
To gently wipe away each tear
When your heart is feeling blue

I prayed He'd bless your labors
Be they great or be they small
But it was for his loving grace
I prayed for most of all.

Judgment

It matters not what caused the deed
That takes one from this life
It matters only that one is gone
From happiness or strife
Propelled into some world unknown
Through tunnels void of light
To a brilliant spot at tunnel's end
That blinds the sense of sight

One hears no voice yet knows the word
That's spoken by the guide
Who leads one on to ones in robes
That stand on either side
Of the brilliant glow of the spot of light
One knows one must abide
The will expressed by the spot of light
Where flows the eternal tide

One feels the love and feels the warmth
And simply wants to stay
But the ones in robes speak to the guide
And the guide seems to say
"The gentle spot of light directs
One toward the record way
You must read the Book of Life and know
That this is Judgment Day."

A Surgeon's Prayer

Green-clad figures darting, turning
In a sterile room aglow
Words of comfort come from him
To the patient there below
Life is hanging like a leaf
From the tree poised to go
Steel blue eyes watch the "signs"
In a way that surgeons know

An uttered prayer from trembling lips
Casts its healing spell
Over the room and all within
In a sense he knows so well
"God grant me wisdom and the skill
To save what you create
Guide my hand in this your task
Let cure then be the fate"

His flashing scalpel then intrudes
Upon created life
The soul retreats inward there
From cruel encroaching light
God's hand did guide the surgeon's knife
In moments fraught with fright
The tempest gone the sea is calm
Once more God's gift is life.

I'm Resting in Sleep

I'm resting in sleep, I did not die
Lift up your heart and don't bother to cry
I have not left you, my presence is nigh
My love is within you, I did not die

When you doubt my presence, when days seem so long
Listen and hear the mockingbird's song
I am the music that thrills your heart
I am the distance between daylight and dark

I'm part of the moon, the stars and the sky
I'm the kiss of the wind and the pine tree's sigh
I'm the gold of the morning and the blue in the sky
Mourn not my passing for I did not die

I know you don't see me and you think I am gone
But I'm right here beside you and you're never alone
I'm the strength of the oak tree and as solid as stone
Fear not, my dear one, and sing not a sad song

I'm resting in sleep, I did not die
So gladden your heart and banish that sigh
I'll always be with you on that you rely
For I am not dead, I did not die.

The Garden

Were I to stand upon the spot
Where Jesus knelt and prayed
To Him above this Father's son
In golden accolades
I'd stand in awe of hallowed ground
Transfixed like blocks of stone
And visualize the "King of Kings"
Who sits upon the throne

I'd feel the love He felt for man
When He walked among us here
I'd go into the lion's den
But my mind would know no fear
I'd weep to see Him bear the cross
He was crucified by sin
I'd dare to kneel upon the spot
And say a prayer to Him.

The Voice of Thunder

I see a white-robed figure
Riding on a cloud
He draws forward ever onward
Followed by a crowd

He speaks with voice of thunder
His words are low and loud
Lightning bolts precede Him
And every head is bowed

There's no mistake! It's judgment!
Where will our poor souls be?
In fire that burns eternal
Or with Him they soar free?

I long to stand upon the spot
Paved with purest gold
And there proclaim my love for Him
Throughout the ages old

I hope to see my loved ones
That went from me before
But most of all I hope to see
My loving spouse once more.

Not Long Enough to Say Good-bye

Life is just a fleeting instant
In the overall plan of time
It's just a simple footstep
On lofty mountains we must climb
But it's from this fleeting instant
A trillion memories are born
Some of them will warm the soul
Others pierce the heart like thorns

Too soon the time for all of us
Shall come for us to say good-bye
When each of us must journey on
To a different place there on high
So hinder not this natural passing
Sever all the bonds that tie
Life is but a fleeting instant
Not long enough to say Good-bye.

Gone like the Wind

Gone like the wind
Are the sands of the past
Nevermore do we see
Gone are the dreams
That will never be dreamed
And all that can never be

Gone are the friends
That once were known
From days of long ago
Gone like the moon
From a cloudless sky
And a breeze that will never blow

Gone like a footstep
That hollow rings
On a path winding slow
Gone is the image
That made the step
And the seeds they were yet to sow

Gone like the wind
Are a thousand schemes
Never on earth to be
Gone is the time
That we have to live
And sights we shall never see.

Across the Miles

If I could wake on Christmas Day
And find you here with me
You'd be a gift I'd love to show
To all the world to see
If I could reach across the miles
And touch your fingertips
If I could feel their warmth and glow
And kiss your smiling lips
I'd know this special holiday
Has been the best that's been
If I could span those endless miles
And hold you once again.

Christmas Vigil

I stand in fields black and silent
Far beneath the midnight sky
Lit by stars like gems that sparkle
In the vastness there on high

A special star appears to glitter
Brighter far than all the rest
The mystery star begins its journey
Slowly moving from the west

The north wind blows sharp and bitter
Making teardrops sting the eye
Across the bleak fields treetops hinder
Its progress causing mournful sighs

Beasts within the barnyard restless
Send up cries of dreadful fright
Heralding that which is to happen
On this glorious night of nights

The miracle birth is ripe to happen
In a manger far away
Prophesied by all the prophets
The King of Kings is born this day!

Die Not in Vain

I have stood on fields of battle
Where ten thousand brave men died
I have lived the din of battle
Seen its anguish and heard its cries
I have heard the shells exploding
And the bullets whizzing by
I have watched their souls ascending
Like wispy shadows toward the sky

I have seen the flag in flutter
Waving proudly from the hill
I've seen its edges stained and tattered
Glorified by brave men's will
I have seen heroic action
In fields of mud and bitter chill
I've heard the angry screaming eagle
From there on high and soaring still

I've heard the sad song of the bugle
Sounding taps there in the trees
I've seen the pristine crosses standing
On the green lawn in the lee
I've heard their muffled voices murmur
Battle cries and trilogies
Departed legions march forever!
Sleep in peace eternally.

Flight of the Lady

A bomber starts to roll in labor on an island across the sea
It lumbers down a long runway and from the earth it struggles
    free
The plane begins a shallow slow climb in a humid pre-dawn
    hour
While all the crew is anxious waiting for instructions from the
    tower

They quickly check the jugs of coffee, rations, snacks, and
    candy bars
And as the ship breaks through dark clouds all eyes on board
    watch the stars
All the engines are purring smoothly as they wing their way to
    war
And every soul on board is thinking of all the comrades gone
    before

It now seems like their journey's ending when in fact it's just
    begun
The pilot's voice in static orders, "All you gunners clear your
    guns"
"Bombardier, set your numbers, for we're about to start our run"
Then the target fast approaches in the land of "Raiding-Hun"

You can see the flak puffs bursting like a black and endless sea
The silent puffs of angry black smoke spewing flak from sea to
    sea
You can hear her skin erupting as the gunners shout with glee
See the Migs on fire and diving sent to hell eternally

Then at last the run is over and the bombs are all away
The gallant ship begins to shudder as she slips and tries to stay
The crew assesses all the damage and it's as plain as plain can
be
The "Lady's" days in flight are over, she will never reach the sea

The pilot's hands now caress her and she flies more steadily
On she limps and on some more as she struggles to set us free
"What's that ahead?" someone is shouting, "Oh my God, this
cannot be!"
"Yes it's true" It's big as life, for they are staring at the sea

Her wings, her tail, her fuselage, and even some of her controls
Are fraught with buckles, rips, and tears by many gaping bullet
holes
This gallant plane her flight life's over but she will always noble
be
She slips at last beneath the dark waves but her deeds will be
retold.

Fighter Pilot

A gloved hand moves in darkness
Forcing throttle to "the wall"
The screaming engines shudder
As tires begin to squall
The fighter's streaking skyward
Belching fire from its tail
In a glorious roar of freedom
And courage that will not fail

The fighter's climbing steeply
Straight up toward a star
Sounds of earth are now behind him
But the destination's far
The fighter streaks at Mach II speed
In straight and level flight
"Missile One" is now away
Fired at "Bogies" in the night

There's no place here for error!
And no time for mistakes!
Gut wrenching turns and blinding rolls
In dives that terror makes!
It's over in a moment
He circles just in case
The welcome call comes at last
"Fighter, return to base"

If ever God did favor
A courageous special breed
It would have to be the "fighter jock"
And his "swift as lightning" steed
So many times he's stared at death
Looked death squarely in the eye
And shrugged death off with gestured hand
"Be gone you ass, I will not die."

Taps

I hear the sound of rifles
They are firing volleys three
For another comrade fallen
That fought to keep us free

A gentle breeze is blowing
Across a grassy hill
I hear a lonely bugle playing
The sound gives me a chill

It's sounding taps at sunset
Another hero's laid to rest
And when they strike the colors
Pride and honor fill my chest

A tiny little teardrop
Fills the corner of my eye
I fight with every ounce of strength
As I try not to cry

When my time on earth is over
And they fire volleys three
Shed not a single teardrop
When the bugle sounds for me.

Friends

Friends I Used to Know

The haunting strains of music
Drift back from long ago
With personal reflections
Recalling friends I used to know
I see their smiling faces
Floating back across the years
Hear their effervescent voices
Sharing plans, dreams, and fears

Enigmatic visions conjured
From inquiring searching minds
That thirst to live life again
From nostalgic happy times
There was Wanda Buck and J. B.
Helen Mutt and Mary Lou
Celestine and Irene
And another one or two

There were picnics, games, and dances
Midnight rides and souvenirs
High school proms and football games
All across those years
Then came the time to say "Good-bye"
And travel far away
But as you go you tell yourself
"I'll travel back again one day"

But years have passed and now at last
The time has come you know
To write a line or make a call
To the friends I used to know
How will they act? What will they say?
When my call at last goes through
I hope I'll hear a voice that says
"Gosh, it's good to hear from you."

The Hand of Friendship

When you're all alone and weary
And you know not what to do
Don't turn your troubles inward
Take down the barriers too

When the cross and pain are heavy
That you are asked to bear
Is a burden that's much too shameful
For you to let yourself to share

Turn toward the hand that reaches
Out to guide your way
Waste not another second
Not a moment to delay

Give us the cross you carry
Let us share the pain
We'll walk along the way there with you
Through stormy bitter rain

One day the sun will shine again
Warm and gentle on your back
And as you sail a calmer sea
You'll set a joyful tack

The cross and pain you used to bear
You'll find are there no more
They're here with us while you sail
As we watch you from the shore.

Morgan's St. Nicholas

Beneath a bold magnolia tree
Near majestic stately walls
Nicholas sleeps eternal peace
And heeds "The Master's" beck and call

The bitter tears will stop you know
As the years pass away
Nick is locked inside your heart
In memory's garden of yesterday

The hands of time on one fine day
Will grant you peace so kind
Your tortured mind and shattered heart
Recall his bark, his kiss, and whine

When setting sun shall touch the sea
And lonely waves on sea walls break
You will hear the red bird's song and know
His love will not forsake

The son of father you now behold
In likeness he does give
Nick's alive and walks about
As long as "Rama" lives.

Jane

The wind still blows in treetops
Birds' wings cleave the sky
The sun still shines on dewdrops
The lake murmurs and sighs

Yet sunsets are a bit less golden
The days a little less bright
Twilight is much more lonely
While stars seem dimmer at night

Moonbeams seem less silver
Bird songs are shy of gay
Our lives are a lot more empty
Since Jane has gone away

Brief was the time of friendship
But daily intensity grew
Her effervescence made our love
But to lose her is painful too

We'll always remember her bright eyes
Her locks of chestnut hair
Her perpetual smile enigmatic
Embellished by complexion fair.

Sandy

Into our lives you drifted
Like silent dreams in sleep
You sang the song of friendship
That stirred our souls so deep
You touched our cheeks with solace
Forbade our hearts to weep
In sickness to God you prayed
Our hardy health to keep

If you stay but a moment with us
In this stormy changing sea
Do not depart in sadness
From ones such as we
We praised your name in song
Sung for the world to see
You enriched our lives forever
With your love abundantly.

Our Friends Ron and Sally

At home in trees beside the lake
They dwell there in the valley
A couple fair this fearless pair
Our friends named Ron and Sally

They live inside a lion's mouth
But are not afraid to dally
They fear not the roaring lion
Our friends named Ron and Sally

With "bully" there their life is rough
They'll give you help to tally
The lion's cave they dare to pass
Our friends named Ron and Sally.

Our Friend Helen

With heart of gold and smile so warm
She'll take you by the hand
She'll walk with you by night or day
Through rough and troubled lands
She is your friend when all seems lost
When life so cruel demands
Your bleeding soul and tortured mind
Be judged by mortal man

She'll listen to your woeful tale
About your life you're telling
She'll pat your hand and tenderly
Dismiss the faults you're selling
A kindred soul of saints long gone
And there's no way foretelling
What gift she'll give next to you
Our much beloved friend Miss Helen.

V

The Specter Rises

You cannot love someone and not be concerned with what is good for them. Other than checkups with her gynecologist and some dental work, Marie had never consulted a doctor. Of course there was one occasion when, for some unknown reason, she developed a trigger finger on her right thumb. This resulted in a minor operation to correct it.

Gene often tried to get Marie to make appointments with his doctor for a physical and an occasional chest X ray, but with no success. She had never been ill a day in her life and didn't need a doctor now, was her philosophy. That didn't keep Gene from trying. He would often feign being upset with her for not taking better care of herself. She knew as well as he did that he was not angry. He could never be angry with her. Concerned yes, very concerned, but never angry. So the months turned into years.

Marie quit smoking in 1991 at Gene's insistence. At least he was successful in that endeavor. Marie was unhappy though and began to gain weight. Gene told her they would work on the weight problem later. He was just happy she had quit. He quit in 1980 and appreciated the health factors of not smoking. They started eating healthy foods and walked long distances almost daily. It was from those long walks around the lake that inspired Gene to write some of his poetry. In fact, some of those poems are in this book.

Still, Marie did not lose the weight she gained by not smoking. Gene noticed she did not have the stamina she once had. She now took naps in the daytime, something she could never do just a few years before. He attributed it to growing older and her added weight. But alas, it later proved not to be the case. Other than the health threat, Gene did not care about the weight. He loved her just as she was. He loved the person he knew was inside that body. He loved her mind, her personality and the goodness he knew was there.

Finally, on July 11, 1997, her health problems manifested themselves in a most shocking way. Gene loved yard work and gardening. It was late in the evening. The summer day was hot and humid and he chose to mow the lawn after the sun set and it cooled off, even if he had to use the tractor lights. While he was checking the equipment, Marie came to him and complained of a terrible headache. She said it was the most painful one she had ever had. Gene told her to take an analgesic and to lie down on the couch. Without a word she turned and entered the house. He sensed that something was wrong because Marie always liked to sit outside and watch him work, but this time she had remained in the house.

About two hours later, he noticed there were no lights in the house and it was completely dark. Gene made a couple more passes with the mower when an uncanny uneasiness seized him. He entered the house. The TV was off, which was unusual. He found "His Lady Rose" on the couch and it was plain she was in trouble. He felt her forehead and she was lightly perspiring. He asked "How are you feeling, love?" She was mumbling but he understood that her head was hurting badly. "Did you take a pain pill?" he inquired. She nodded her head in the affirmative. Gene asked her what she had taken. Marie retorted in what sounded like German. He knew a little German, but he didn't know that phrase. Once more he inquired, "What did you take, dear?" She again replied "sluffenslagen." The reply totally alarmed Gene. Marie was clearly getting agitated. He tried something else. This time he asked her to show him what she had taken. By now he noted an unsteadiness in her. Marie went to her purse, took out a small bottle of over-the-counter medication and excitedly stabbed her finger at the label of non-aspirin pain medication and repeated the term, "Sluffenslagen, sluffenslagen."

Gene was now thoroughly alarmed and was apprehensive. He gently led her to the couch where they sat down. His pulse was racing and his blood pressure was climbing as was evidenced by the feeling of a band around his head. His cheeks were flushed and his head ached slightly. He put his arms around her and said, "Darling, you are frightening me. If you are joking, please stop. If you are not joking, we need help." With that Marie just melted into his arms and said. "Please hold me." He recognized what appeared to be symptoms of a stroke and the weight of the world seemed to settle on his shoulders. He could not lose her. She must not die!

The illness had happened at the house of a friend who was traveling in Europe. Gene and Marie were caring for the house and their dogs. Gene knew he could transport Marie to the local hospital much faster than an ambulance could be summoned. He was familiar with the red tape of transport preparation they had to follow. But he could not leave the house open and unattended. He called another friend who arrived forthwith and took responsibility for the house and dogs, while Gene put Marie into the car. It was a new sports car and could travel swiftly.

Gene had been trained in high speed chases and pursuit driving by the North Carolina Highway Patrol many years ago. Once you learn the skill, you never forget it. In six minutes they were near the hospital some eight miles away. Gene didn't trust the small "staging" hospital much and as he approached the major highway to Houston, he was ready to turn the speeding car south. By some miracle fate stayed his hand and he entered the emergency room driveway. Gene took Marie into the emergency room immediately as she was still ambulatory with help. He placed her in a chair and loudly informed the attendant Marie was suffering symptoms of a stroke and needed immediate emergency attention.

The attendant, schooled in spinning red tape, inquired about insurance, its type and coverage. "We can do that later," retorted Gene. "But, sir . . . " she stated and before she could utter another word Gene exploded by slamming the insurance cards on her desk and shouted "Move it, woman. Get a doctor out here, this woman is going into shock!" With those words he was at Marie's side. She was still lucid but her eyes were glazed and her face was bathed in sweat. In an instant, two medics and a gurney were in the lobby. The nurse quickly saw why Gene was so excited and ordered Marie loaded onto the gurney. She was immediately assigned to the treatment room.

They had arrived at the hospital around 8:00 P.M. Gene was at Marie's side. The doctor on duty was standing at the treatment desk and several medical persons were fussing from time to time with Marie. However, nothing major was being done. One hour later Marie appeared to be entering a catatonic stage. She was not responding as well as before to Gene's reassuring words of love. He noticed Marie had dropped her head; her eyes were completely glazed and perspiration was streaming off her face. She had now been in the treatment room some ninety minutes. They had slowly undressed her. Gene had removed her jewelry and taken control of her clothing. After two hours, they finally put an IV drip into her and had catheterized her. She was now admitted. Gene continuously alerted the doctor and nurse to the fact Marie was sweating profusely and was not responding to conversation. Her pulse was weak and racing. He pleaded with the doctor to do something for her but was told they could not treat until they diagnosed. They couldn't diagnose until they had a CAT scan.

Finally at 10:45 they wheeled the gurney out into the aisle and started toward X ray. At that moment Gene noticed she had gone into convulsions. Her body was heaving into the air completely off the gurney. It did so several times before action was taken. Gene went toward the doctor. "Do something now!" he demanded. "Oh she is just having a little stroke," the doctor calmly stated as he leaned against the desk. The gurney had stopped and finally one medic was pounding on Marie's chest. He appeared to be trying to administer C.P.R. The heart monitor alarmed and flat-lined. That was it!

Gene lunged for the doctor who was still leaning against the desk. As he did so two medics tried to restrain him. He threw one across the room and the other retreated. He was at the doctor by this time. "You S.O.B., act like a doctor or I will own you and this hospital!" he screamed. The doctor ducked and came to life. He was at Marie's side in an instant. He ordered an injection and the life-saving defibrillation paddles. Gene's blood pressure had exploded. The nurses had pleaded with him to let the medical personnel do their job. He knew he could do nothing for her now and relinquished control of the situation. He was taken to the adjoining room where his blood pressure was monitored. It had climbed to 210/140. He could hear every beat of his heart thunder in his ears. Gene's face was blood red, hot and perspiring as each heartbeat sent stabbing pains to his head. He could care less. He thought Marie was dead and so he wanted to die too. A sweet little nurse came to his side and asked if he took medication. "Yes, I do," he stated. With that she helped Gene contact his neighbor, who brought the medication to the hospital for him to take.

By now they had revived Marie. As is the case in some seizures, she was reacting violently. What Gene had threatened to do to the procrastinating, so-called "angels of mercy," Marie was doing. There were seven men trying to hold her down. Gene did not know where they came from. They had reluctantly let him back into the treatment room by telling him Marie had revived. He saw Marie kick and one two-hundred-pound man went flying. Then another and another. She was now vocal and kicking with all her might. They could not hold her hands. Gene thought about her dentures and asked if they had removed them. He was informed they had gotten the lower plate but she was still in possession of the uppers. He knew the danger of her swallowing those things and he was by her side. In a short while he had calmed her but the dentures were another matter. She wasn't going to allow them to be removed. But as usual, he finally calmed her enough to allow him to remove them. From then on things improved.

Marie was wheeled to the X ray room where the CAT scan was performed. Everyone was now much calmer. They were also more alert and active. It seemed like an eternity before she was returned to the treatment room. An hour or two later, the doctor had the results. She would have to be moved to a better equipped hospital. Marie was suffering from a lesion in her brain and needed a contrast MRI immediately. She was in a very grave condition. Gene's heart was broken but he knew he had to be there for her. She had recovered from the seizure and the cardiac arrest and wanted to talk to Gene. He told her they were taking her to the medical center at Houston, by ambulance. She wanted Gene to take her in the car. Gene explained she would need paramedics with her for the 100-mile drive and assured her he would be there as fast as possible. At 2:20 A.M., they moved Marie to Methodist Hospital in Houston.

Gene hurried home, bathed, and took care of emergencies. He left as soon as humanly possible. It was a terrible night for driving and he could not drive fast. He had not driven in downtown Houston for several years and was not now familiar with it. A lot of construction had been completed and was still going on. This destroyed all the old landmarks he was familiar with. At any rate he finally found Methodist Hospital and hurried to Marie's room. She was still awake at 4:00 A.M. and anxious. Gene set about calming her. He held her as best he could under the circumstances and reassured her she would be all right, believing they were in the best of hands. For a stroke, Marie was not experiencing any numbness or weakness on either side. This concerned Gene and at the same time gave him hope that all would be well.

The next day an MRI was done but the doctors were not that helpful. Marie seemed to feel all right. They had started giving her

Dilantin, an anti-seizure drug she was comfortable with, which seemed to help.

When Marie first became ill, Gene had called her brother Leon and his wife, Melinda. Knowing they would sound the alarm for the whole clan and thereby save Gene valuable time spent in calling each one individually. He should have known what would happen next, but he gave the possibility no thought. Sure enough, a phone call came and it was Melinda. "I am in Houston and I am lost." She had flown into George Bush Airport, rented a car and had driven downtown on the advice of the leasing attendant. She had done well though, because she was only blocks from the hospital. Gene gave her directions and in minutes she was there. He met her at the parking garage and took her to Marie's room.

"I will either stay here at the hospital or go to your house and take care of things there, whichever is the most beneficial to you." said Melinda. Since their friend, Sally, had been caring for their dog as well as their friend's dogs, Melinda could now relieve Sally and she could manage the two houses until they were once more home again. Melinda said, "I will stay a week or as long as you need me."

Melinda and Gene stayed at the hospital with Marie until late evening. They kissed Marie good-bye and drove north. Melinda followed Gene in her rented car as Gene led the way through the maze of street and highway construction currently going on in Houston. Gene knew Melinda had not eaten so he pulled off the highway to a restaurant where they hurriedly ordered a meal and devoured it posthaste. Both were hungry but still made small conversation politely while dining.

Gene had always wished for a sister, but had none. This wonderful lady who was many years his junior, was as close to being a sister as anyone was ever going to get. As a sister he loved her dearly, and he felt the feeling was mutual. Gene first gained respect for Melinda early in her marriage to his brother-in-law, Leon, when his father-in-law, Russell Hughes, was critically ill.

Melinda was a "take-charge" person who did things for Russell in his illness that most blood children would have balked at doing. Any way, Melinda stayed for a week and was a tremendous help to Gene and Marie.

The following day the doctors told Gene that Marie was doing fine and said he could take her home on Wednesday. They said she had suffered a lesion in the back of the brain, on the right side. After discharge, her doctor did not want to see her for a month. They started systematically decreasing the Dilantin, and finally removed her from the drug altogether.

Gene gladly took Marie home. They started walking again but Marie was not as strong as she had been before. She complained of headaches constantly. Gene called her doctor but he was not concerned. The headaches gradually worsened but were bearable. On August 13, 1997, Marie went for her final checkup. Again, the doctor was not concerned about the headaches. He blamed them on Dilantin and said the drug remains in the system. But Marie's headaches kept becoming more severe and this worried Gene immensely. He remembered how her condition had begun.

Finally, Gene had enough. He called his own doctor, whom he had used for twenty-five years. On August 29, 1997, they went to Houston to keep the appointment with this new medicine man, who thoroughly examined Marie, asked them to reiterate her symptoms and describe again the seizure she had suffered two or three times.

Bob turned to Gene and said, "Gene, something stinks about this whole thing. First off, a stroke always produces some kind of numbness, or weakness, on one side or the other. She had none of that. Secondly, you never remove a patient from Dilantin for at least a year, when they have suffered a seizure."

The doctor then examined Marie's eyes with a lighted instrument. After searching both eyes for several minutes he turned to Gene and said, "Gene, I am seeing severe cranial pressure present with profuse bleeding into the retina from both vein and artery. I want her to have a complete eye examination with refraction immediately. I'll make the appointment."

With that remark he went to work and a few minutes later sent them to a nearby ophthalmologist, where the examination was immediately done. The ophthalmologist confirmed Bob's diagnosis and immediately sent them back to Bob's office, where he was waiting for them.

Gene had been going to this doctor for years and they had become friends and were on a first name basis. Gene could tell that Bob was greatly concerned. He turned to face both of them and said, "Gene, Marie's condition is very grave. She must enter the hospital immediately and you must take her there for it is faster. I will pre-admit her but I want to warn you, there is no assurance she will live until you get her there. Even if she does, she could go blind or die on the way, during the night, or tomorrow. The most common thing to cause this is a brain tumor and that could have been thrown there by a cancer somewhere in her body. Go now and I will gather a team of specialists and we will be there immediately."

Gene was shaking inside but he did not let on to Marie. He quickly, but carefully took Marie the two blocks to the hospital. True to his word, Bob had pre-admitted her and she went directly to a room. Within two minutes Bob was there with a neurologist. He examined Marie and confirmed Bob's findings. She was immediately given a chest and a skull X ray, followed by a contrast MRI; Bob had called the best MRI technician he could find, and the technician came to the hospital.

Gene was waiting in Marie's room when Bob came back. He was pale and grim. Gene instantly knew the news was bad from the expression on his face. "Gene, she has a tumor on her left lung and another on the outer rib cage. There are thirty-two tumors in her brain, with a larger one on the brain stem. I will almost bet you they are malignant. I have a radiologist coming in to do a needle aspiration on the tumor in the lung and a brain surgeon to release the cranial pressure. She is now in intensive care. It will be a while but I will get you in to see her as soon as I can. Bear in mind the chemical treatment we have started itself could kill her. Just pray," said Bob.

Gene went to the third floor waiting room. Before long Bob joined him. As busy as he was, he stayed with Gene until 10:30 that night. He treated Gene for high blood pressure and made him comfortable. Bob then received the technical diagnosis on the tumors. They were malignant!

Around 4:00 A.M., they allowed Gene to be with "his lady." They closed the drapes and had their privacy. The brain surgeon came and told Gene he was going home because he would not dare operate on Marie. It would kill her. Gene went back to his one love. Marie was not asleep. They both knew how grim the outlook was and they started to cope with Marie's mortality for the first time. They discussed final plans they had never discussed before and Gene surprisingly became enlightened. Heretofore, Marie had never talked about herself, or of her little "likes and dislikes." For example, Gene knew her like a good book—but he never knew her favorite church hymn, where she wanted to be buried or any of her final wishes. She had never discussed the subject. Since he was eighteen years her senior, they just assumed he would go first and they planned their lives around that scenario, never dreaming that Marie could have a life-threatening disease or even die first. How stupid of them! Well, he knew now and started action immediately.

Marie responded to the chemical treatment. She was on high doses of steroids and anti-seizure medication. Marie tolerated the medicine well. She was discharged and went home after a few days with instructions to make an appointment with radiology oncology the next week for radiation of the brain. The appointment was made and treatment began immediately. Marie was herself again. She was jovial, smiling and good-natured. From her actions, you would not know she was so gravely ill. However, Gene could see the slowness with which she accomplished those actions and he also noted the sluggishness of her mental capacity. Gosh, Marie's mind had been like a "screaming speed computer" before she suffered the attack. Well, that had changed; but Gene was determined to deal with whatever fate threw at them. He was practical about it, but he was upbeat for her sake.

The daily 200-mile round trip to the hospital for radiation therapy was a drain on both of their energies. In conversation with Marie's old friend Beverly, she had suggested they stay in Houston during the week and live at her house. Marie decided to take her up on the offer and arrangements were made. It was much nicer than commuting. Their friend and neighbor, Sally, cared for their home and pet. It was a pleasant workable solution.

Weeks went by with radiation therapy daily during the week and then home to the lake for the glorious restful weekends. Marie was still able to walk and get around. They dined out on several occasions. Their fruit trees were just loaded with fruit. The July Elberta peaches were sweet, ripe, and absolutely delicious. Together they cleaned, prepared and froze the fresh fruit, eating several peaches while preparing them. It was fun and at times they forgot her illness. Gene found himself stealing long moments just looking at Marie. He did so when she was not looking. God, he loved her! What on earth would he do with his life if these treatments were not successful. He would not allow himself to think of that now.

They were both anxious for the results of the radiation which was making Marie weaker. In the meantime, Marie underwent surgery to place a porta-cath into her chest as an access port for the pending chemotherapy they were anticipating. She weathered that fine. It was her first experience with invasive surgery. Marie was starting to feel like an old trouper from the TV series, *Chicago Hope*.

Good news! The recent MRI of her brain indicated all of the

brain tumors had vanished, except a small one on the brain stem. They were going to watch that during chemotherapy and if necessary, radiate it again. Bad news! The chemotherapy was making Marie extremely ill. She couldn't eat and was vomiting constantly. Gene felt so sorry for her he cried frequently—but always in private. Oh, how he wished he could take the discomfort for her! He prayed constantly for hours at a time. While spending long hours at Marie's bedside he began jotting down his feelings in poetry form as a pastime. When at home on the lake he found himself walking the floor at all hours of the night. When in Houston, he would lie awake thinking of what apparently lay ahead. He was struggling with his sanity and the horrible prospect that he might have to go on alone. It was frightening to anticipate the horrible loneliness that would be his without her, the empty bed beside him, the hollow rooms of their home without her presence. . . . *Stop that!* he thought to himself. She wasn't gone yet and they were going to fight.

In the meantime, the oncologist had prescribed oral medication and a special formulated suppository for the nausea and they were working. Marie could not eat, though. Even the smell of food made her sick to her stomach. Gene was wracking his brain, trying to come up with something she found appealing and that she could keep in her stomach. At times, some worked and some didn't. The chemotherapy went on. They conducted an abdominal contrast MRI on Marie. Thank God! The chemicals had reduced the lung tumor some forty-five percent. However, the tumor on her rib cage had now destroyed three ribs and showed no signs of slowing down. They had slowed the brain threat and lung threat. *But what about the rib cage?* More chemotherapy.

Poor darling! Marie was growing weaker, unable to hold anything on her stomach. They tried all of the nutrition supplements. None worked. Her hearing and vision were both damaged. All of her hair came out and she was completely bald. Worse yet, she was now losing all of her body hair. Marie put up a good front and tried to pretend it didn't bother her that much, if Gene could stand it. No problem with Gene. He just wanted "his lady" any way he could have her. Bev made Marie some stylish head gear to cover her baldness and Marie loved them. She wore them constantly.

The stress and strain was now taking its toll on Gene also. He "couldn't sleep for worry," so he wrote. He was always lying beside her or sitting near the bed. When the stress became too great, he would pace. She slept a lot now. On one occasion they were at the lake and Gene was looking out an upstairs window near their bedroom. There was a full moon shining through the tree branches. The conditions caused strange shadow formations to appear on the lawn. It inspired him to write a poem about the ghostly shadows and then several on the same topic spilled out of his mind into copy. A selection of some of those poems is set forth below.

My Agony

She bravely held my hand that day
When the doctor came to tell
The words that were to break my heart
Condemning hopes as well

No chance for tomorrow!
No more dreams to dream
Beloved Marie is being called
To a better place it seems

My God, how I have loved her
Warmed by her sunny smile
Soothed by the touch of her fingertips
Through countless hours and miles

I cannot live without her
Life's over when she goes
For now we'll bless the hours we have
'Til the book of life will close.

Night Vigil

Patches of moonlight lying on the ground
Casting specters onto the view
Of sleepless nights and endless hours
Where happy thoughts are few

I know the "reaper" stalks the scene
His sign is all about
As terror grips my aching heart
I all but hear him shout

He calls the name of "My Marie"
And rides grim beams of light
That form the scene of this nightmare
And haunt my soul with fright

"You shall have her not!" I shout at him
As his gray steed gallops by
I quickly go back to her side
And listen for her sigh

Once again she's in my arms
Upon this bed of love
Once more the "reaper" passes by
Repulsed by Him above.

The Pale Horse

A pale horse came prancing
Slowly walking to her side
He pawed the air around her
And beckoned her to ride
But she refused to mount him
She turned her face away
The pale horse then vanished
She had refused to play
I know he will return again
Inviting her to ride
I hope she will again refuse
And stay here by my side.

VI

The Beginning of the End

Between October and December of 1997, Marie was in and out of the hospital several times. Bob was on the board of directors at the hospital and although he didn't say, Gene felt it was the reason Marie was placed in a two-person room and then no one else was admitted to that room. Such action made the room a private room and as such Gene could stay with her at night, as well as the day. Stay he did. In the early days Marie was somewhat ambulatory. Gene would help her to the bathroom and assist her in bathing. He loved to be of help to her and she appeared to love having him there to help. Gene managed to get some food down her and she was holding her own. They vacillated back and forth from home to the hospital. Marie was having more and more trouble walking. She now used a walker and moved more slowly. Gene never rushed her and allowed her to maintain her independence as long as humanly possible. He knew what the lack of mobility and independence would mean to him in the same situation. When at home Marie could get up and down the stairs to their bedroom slowly with the help Gene was glad to give.

It was early October and the weekend was sunny. Marie was sitting on the front porch, enjoying the pleasant weather. Their garden had been neglected due to Marie's illness. Gene was pulling up pepper plants and was trying to tidy the garden, but just once he turned the wrong way as he pulled—and felt something give way in his back. It hurt but he did not pay much attention to it.

The following week in Houston, he noted that the pain in his back was getting worse. He could hardly walk. One evening while sitting on the couch at Bev's house, he could not move his legs or get up off the couch. Beverly came to his assistance and moved his legs for him. That seemed to help and he was able to move but with great difficulty. Bev gave him a back brace to put on, which helped a lot. Gene went to the doctor, who suspected a cracked vertebra. Sure enough, the doctor was right. It was broken in three places. In time, the back mended, but Gene never relinquished Marie's care to anyone during the incident and was able to do what he had to do despite the pain of his back.

It was now November. Gene had kept Marie's family completely informed of her condition. They were all planning on celebrating Thanksgiving at Gene and Marie's home on the lake that year. November moved along at a rapid rate in spite of Marie's long suffering. It was almost Thanksgiving and Marie's family had started to arrive. Her brother Wayne from Oklahoma with his wife Martha; her brother Leon and wife Melinda from South Carolina; her brother Kenneth, and sister Ella Mae from Arkansas. All were spending Thanksgiving with Marie and Gene. Marie could no longer climb the stairs. Gene and her brothers moved part of the living room into the bedroom and the bed came down into the living room. Gene had purchased a large screen TV for Marie as she was having trouble seeing their old TV due to vision loss. Gene rented a wheelchair for Marie and she was getting around quite well with it. Thanksgiving came and went. Marie was trying to move from the chair to the couch one day shortly thereafter, when a loud popping noise was heard. Gene thought she had slipped a hip joint out of place; but from that day forward, Marie never walked again. Gene rented a patient lift from a medical supply house which was used to move Marie from the wheelchair to the bed and from the bed to the wheelchair. It helped also in toilette.

It became extremely painful for Marie to be moved or rolled over in bed. Gene knew this meant something was very wrong. He called Marie's oncologist, who pre-admitted Marie to the hospital. The ambulance came and transported her, Gene close behind. When they arrived, tests were conducted and it was determined Marie had a broken hip. They had been warned that the cancer would make the bones brittle. The MRI also indicated Marie had a large tumor on both femur bones in her legs. That was truly bad news as such a diagnosis is a death sentence. The doctors felt surgery was the only answer.

The surgeon performed the operation on Marie's hip and thigh bones on the evening of December 2, 1997. All attempts at rehabilitation failed and Marie never walked or moved her lower body again. The pain was so severe she had to be placed on a morphine pump. The long vigil began with sleepless nights and the agony of watching someone you love waste away before your eyes. By then Marie's sister, Jean, was there to help and she turned out to be a walking saint, who cared for Marie tirelessly.

Gene was spending forty-eight to ninety-six hours at a time at Marie's bedside, unable to rest or sleep. In the long night hours he wrote constantly about the horror and agony of pending death, of pending loneliness. The destruction of dreams. For your appreciation, here now are those personal thoughts that were his constant companion as he struggled with "His Lady's" pending death.

The Cancer Dragon

Oh God! The pain is screaming!
It bounces off the wall
Helplessly, I stand about
And press the "nurse's call"

Eternity then passes
Before someone appears
To reassure my doubtful mind
And wipe away her tears

The monster that devours her
Dragon of ages old
Would that I could slay it
And be her knight so bold

Better men than I have tried
Sir Galahads today
Have failed to slay the dragon
What more is there to say?

The Vigil Ship

With the windows tightly shuttered
Against the darkened gloom
Starts the nightly vigil
In a lonely silent room
The hours will slowly fade away
With the ticking of the clock
When the "vigil ship" sails again
From the fading daytime dock

We'll drift upon a sea of pain
Together she and I
I'll hold her hand and stroke her cheek
She'll know not that I cry
The tears that fall upon her hand
Are mine and mine alone
I die each day to see her thus
Would God but take her home

Forsake us not in time of strife
Our bodies racked with pain
When breaking hearts are cleansed and washed
By tears that fall like rain
Lift the spirit! Set it free!
That it may to You fly
Let every soul that dares to pray
Feel Your presence nigh.

The Morning After

Sunlight greets the morning
That's finally come to stare
At tiny little puffballs
Drifting in the air

A solitary bluebird flits
A nervous jerking sight
Who's lagged behind the exit
Of the migrating flight

The tall tree standing stately
With limbs stark and bare
It sways and bends before the wind
Free from every care

I find that I resent these things
Because she cannot see
Forever bound an invalid
Never to be free

Nonetheless the beauty's there
This I can't deny
So I admire those moments
While a teardrop stings my eye.

Buffy's Rose

The day was full of troubles
In Rose's sick bedroom
My heart was sore and broken
Because her life must end so soon

It was on a Thursday evening
When friend Buffy came to call
Rose's pain had set me walking
Up and down the noisy hall

In Buffy's hand was a treasure
A solitary long-stemmed rose
With a blossom pink and perfect
That brought the image to a close

In Rose's eyes we watched the pleasure
That was beaming on Rose's face
And both we knew that the moment
Gave a meaning to the place

Such a friend is hard to come by
Perfect timing and perfect taste
When even death was stayed a moment
Buffy ran the perfect race.

Angels

Hark! Angels present
On gleaming silver wings
As they hover around the bedside
With golden harps that ring

A brilliant glow surrounds her
And encompasses the room
While "The Virgin Mother" cometh
Beneath the light of winter's moon

She reaches down so gently
To touch the face of my Marie
Though my heart is filled with sadness
She makes my blind eyes see

The "King of Kings" is calling!
"His Will" must be done!
His might is ever present
In the burning of the sun

I cannot help but wonder
When the morning finally comes
Will my love still be with me
Or will her race in life be run?

I'll Know You're Gone

Oh my darling! How I love you!
How I'll mourn when you are gone
How my heart will break with sorrow
When the angels take you home

Many nights I sat beside you
Prayed with you and held your hand
I saw your pain and watched you suffer
While longing for a better land

I don't know why you have to suffer
Or why your life is filled with pain
Or why God should take you from me
And why should I on earth remain

I only know that life is over
That the end now won't be long
I'll feel your presence with me forever
But I will also know you're gone.

Caring Evermore

How distinctly I remember
The dreary month of bleak December
When the angels came a'calling
Calling at my humble door

While my loved one lay a'dying
And I in mournful crying
Heard the angels come a'flying
Flying through the shuttered core

They had come to bear her homeward
While the hands of time marched onward
Lo, the trumpets set to blaring
Blaring 'cross the lonely moor

How their silver wings were glaring
While into her face I staring
Saw my loved one greatly caring
Caring for me evermore.

During these agonizing hours, days and weeks, two people came into Gene's life who meant the world to him. There are no words to express just how much those two added to the support, meaning and understanding of this horrifying experience he was exposed to. Over the years he had lost friends, relatives, and even his own parents. He had personally faced death many times. He always came away whole and unscathed. This monster he could not fight, much less win the fight against it. One is at its mercy.

One of those people was Marie's sister, Jean. When it was apparent that Marie was dying, she came and stayed until the end. Gene saw her go hour after hour without sleep. Standing at Marie's bedside, rubbing and massaging Marie's painful limbs. It seemed to give Marie relief and she begged for that comfort constantly. Poor Marie! She grew more pale and weaker by the hour. Since Jean's arrival on the scene, Gene was getting a little more rest. They took turns sitting beside Marie and caring for her. Every time the morphine alarm sounded, they ran for help. Neither wanted Marie to suffer any more than was absolutely necessary.

Jean had lost her husband to bone cancer just a few years before. She was no newcomer to the suffering field. She had experience with the problems that are common with cancer patients. Jean was uncanny when it came to tricking Marie into eating something nutritious. It was this unselfish kind of action that inspired Gene to write the poem "Jean" which will appear further along in this chapter.

The other person referred to earlier as being such a help to Gene was Father Bob. Father Bob is the loving, endearing title given to the Right Reverend Robert Parker, the vicar of St. Luke's Episcopal Church. Gene met Father Bob at a Christmas party which was given by a neighbor some two years prior to Marie's illness. He conversed with him and was much impressed by Father Bob and his vivacious wife, Garnet. Gene knew several members of Father Bob's congregation and had heard nothing but marvelous things about the minister, so, naturally, when Gene saw the need for a minister, he turned to Father Bob. He was not disappointed. Father came to their home and to the hospital where he ministered to the needs of Marie. He was later to play the major role in Gene's returning to church as he should have. It was this man's devotion to God's work that inspired Gene to write the poem "Father Bob," which appears in this chapter, along with the poem "Jean."

Jean

When the hours are hard and endless
And the nighttime vigil's long
I often contemplate my blessings
As my soul sings its song
While the notes soar to heaven
On the wings of a prayer
My wounds from daily living
Are starkly raw and bare

While I sit at the bedside
Of my loved one gravely ill
The winds of doubt are blowing
With a frigid Arctic chill
As my troubled mind rehearses
The sad macabre scene
I'm thankful for the help of
My loving sister Jean.

Father Bob

When the night seems the darkest
And daily hours are so long
When our hearts are filled with sadness
Somehow he finds a song

When the soul cries out in anguish
Our shoulders shake from tear and sob
One can always count on comfort
From our beloved "Father Bob"

You can feel God's Holy Presence
When his hands upon you lay
And surely God rejoices
When he kneels with us to pray

When his work is finally over
And our Savior calls him home
I believe he'll dwell forever
Near God's shining golden throne.

VII

A Painful End

The date was December 17, 1997. For several days Marie had not chosen to talk very much. Talking seemed to cause her more pain. It was apparent she had become addicted to the morphine. There were periods of profuse sweating and the feeling she was burning up, which caused her to plead for a fan. The little angels in rehabilitation had brought a fan to her room. At times she was cross and her speech was more slurred. There were other times when she did not respond to questions. It was apparent she was deteriorating rapidly. Since December 4, 1997, she had been going daily to X ray for radiation on her pelvis and legs in an effort to shrink the tumors. Also, they wanted to strengthen the bones and they thought radiation would do that.

It was a very painful process for Marie to be moved from her bed to a gurney and from the gurney to the treatment table. After the treatment the process had to be reversed. On this date, at 10:20 P.M., Marie and Gene were alone. Her sister had taken a break. Marie clearly exclaimed, "Will you talk to me?" Gene responded by saying, "Darling, I will talk to you any place, any time and about anything." "I don't want to take any more treatments, Gene. I am so tired and I want to go home." Gene thought she meant home to the lake but after talking further he learned she meant she wanted to go to heaven. It was at this point that Marie spelled out all the things she wanted done. She had already planned her funeral, picked the casket and the funeral was pre-paid. But now she was picking hymns and disposing of her personal jewelry. She spelled out every detail. Gene's heart was breaking because he knew she was telling him she was leaving him.

When Jean came back, Marie again repeated her wishes and stated she wanted Jean to hear what those wishes were. Gene had been holding her in his arms. She said, "I am tired now and I want to lie back." Gene slowly eased her onto the hospital bed. He fought to hold back the tears. Jean was dumbfounded. Marie spoke very little after that. Gene excused himself and went to the public bathroom to be completely out of the hospital room. There he cried uncontrollably for a long time. After refreshing himself, he returned to Marie's room. Her lips formed the words, "I love you," and he almost lost his composure again. Jean sat and stared, as if in shock. Neither of them slept that night.

The next day Marie's oncologist came by and discussed her decision with Gene. The oncologist had learned that Gene refused any further treatment on Marie's part that morning. He was in agreement. New tumors had formed under the skin adjacent to the large tumor on the rib cage. A needle aspiration proved it to be malignant. It was mutually agreed Marie would go home under the care of a hospice attendant for comfort and would undergo no more life-saving treatments. She was going home to die, by her own request and decision. When their eyes met, they both knew why she was quitting. Gene's health, too, was failing fast from the strain. He had lost forty pounds and was two sizes smaller. Marie saw that and she was not going to let it get any worse. With her eyes she told Gene she had to go and he had to stay. Gene didn't care how much weight he lost or even if he lived after she went. He cared only about Marie. Prior to this state of affairs, they had long talks, vowing their undying love for each other. They had lain in each other's arms and talked all night, especially after Gene moved their bed into the living room when she could no longer climb the stairs. They knew even then that the end was fast approaching, that all the medical procedures had been just attempts at buying her some more time. But, had it been quality time?

Marie was home once more on December 20, 1997. The hospice attendant had been contacted while she was still in the hospital. Her home-type hospital bed was all set up and waiting for her, prior to her arrival. They brought the morphine pump with her in the ambulance. She was all set to ride out the storm until God's final summons arrived. Unfortunately, just as her luck had been running bad for months, it struck again. The damn morphine pump malfunctioned and the hospice company made an immediate decision to transport her to Huntsville for hospitalization. The EMT's were still at the house; after just one hour at home she was off again. Marie was devastated. She was so tired and now the pain was growing worse without the medication. In no time they were at Huntsville Memorial.

Treatment began again in an effort to wean her from the pump and place her on patches and oral medication. This would allow Gene and the assigned home nurse to administer the medication and thereby keep her comfortable. But again, bad luck was the dominating factor. In their zeal to do a good job, the medical personnel reduced the medication too quickly. Just as Gene suspected, Marie was more addicted then everyone thought. Having been a federal agent in his past life and having conducted many narcotics investigations, he recognized addiction symptoms immediately. That day turned out to be one of the darkest days of Gene's life. It haunts him even now. Although he knew he was acting properly for Marie's sake, the results were emotionally devastating. At first Marie was extremely restless. Then she started pulling at the porta-cath and the IVs as if to remove them. Gene kept trying to calm her but could not. He called the attending nurse who administered a sedative. The sedative reacted in conjunction with the morphine present and Marie became mildly violent. She was aggressive and continuously called Gene. Even though he answered it did not quiet her. Gene was totally exhausted and finally stopped answering. Marie became more violent. She could only move her upper body but that was enough to cause major problems. Gene called the nurse again. The nurse applied restraints. Marie blamed Gene and begged him to remove the restraints. When he would not she became very abusive vocally. Gene knew it was the medication that was causing the problem. He had never heard Marie use curse words before in his life with her and knew this was not "His Lady" talking. Nevertheless, the name calling hurt. Marie was using "guilt trip" type of sentences and questions, such as, "What if I died tonight?" Gene's only reply was, "I would be devastated." Devastated he was. Nothing, in all of his years on earth, hurt like the incidents of that night hurt and nothing has ever haunted him more. Of all the things to have happen to a couple as much in love as they, this would forever cause him to wonder if he could have acted differently or done more for her.

With the advent of dawn and the coming of the doctor early next morning, came relief. The attending physician increased the morphine from the pump and combined that with oral morphine. That did the trick and Marie was out of restraints. Her disposition improved. Gene was able to get her to eat a little from time to time. Daily they reduced the pump-dispensed medication and increased the oral medication. They had also placed a patch on Marie's body.

Leon and Melinda arrived from South Carolina for Christmas. They were relieving Gene at the hospital so he could get some proper rest. Jean was able to get some rest also. In a few days Marie was home for the final time. It was impossible to tell anyone how happy Gene was to have "His Lady" home once more. He knew in his heart, from observations he had made, that Marie had less than two weeks left with him. Gene knew her well and thought he should let all of their close friends know she was home so they could have a chance to say their last good-byes. So he did.

Two such friends were Judy and Charlie Helmer. Gene and Judy had gone to school together at Texas A&M. They had met and become fast friends. Soon thereafter they introduced Marie and Charlie and the friendship was off and running. The couples were together almost every weekend after that. First at one house and then the other with their lively card games. It wasn't just Judy and Gene's friendship; they all grew to love each other. Gene thought as much of Charlie as he did of Judy. Judy thought as much of Marie as she did Gene. The same was true of Marie and Charlie. It was a marvelous friendship that lasted twenty-three years. The Helmer children were small when the adult foursome met. Gene and Marie watched those children grow into adulthood, go through school, marry and have children of their own. They shared their trauma of growing right along with their parents. In reiteration, it was a wonderful, loving and rewarding friendship.

As soon as Gene called, Judy and Charlie came. Judy came several times thereafter alone as Charlie had to work. Thank God they were able to be with Marie when she could still respond to them. Although in severe pain and with her mind clouded with the heavy doses of the pain-killing drugs, Marie was clearly pleased to see them. She laboriously attempted to converse with them. Judy was there at the end and most felt that Marie knew. Gene knew Marie was aware of Judy's presence. He had learned to read her eyes.

Marie's good friend, Beverly, was also there near the end and came back with her daughter Tammy to assist after the end came. It was extremely tough for Beverly, particularly when she read some of the poetry Gene had written about Marie's illness. Gene would never have allowed her to read it if he had only known what an impact it would have upon her. God knows he never intended anyone to suffer for or by anything he did. There were so many who came that week, such as Ron and Sally, Iris and Warren, A. J. and Irene, Pete and Helen B. as well as Jack and Helen M. Gene's brother also came and was able to speak with Marie before the final end.

The family had agreed not to exchange gifts this year because of Marie's illness. They did, however, have a large dinner. Marie only ate a few bites. She was lucid and responsive. She talked a little more. The attending nurse lived close by and was there in just a few minutes when she was called. Her name was Eunice Jordan and she wore a little angel around her neck. If ever a saintly person walked this earth, Eunice was it. Gene had never before met anyone quite like her. Her voice was calm and soothing, yet penetrating at the same time. Gene firmly believed she was an angel herself. She was certainly angelic with Marie and that's what mattered to Gene. Without the strength and guidance of Eunice in those final days, Gene knew he could not have made it. He never worried anymore about Marie's pain or her personal hygienic care. Eunice was always there. She had warned Gene that Marie would go into, what is called, the dying stage. She explained that Marie would increasingly become less responsive and in all probability, would slip into a coma or just not respond at all. Oh, God—how he dreaded that!

Marie was starting to continuously slow down in her response to the family. It was now December 27, 1997. As the days clicked off her responses lessened. Leon had returned to South Carolina, leaving Jean and Mae. Jean was uncanny in her ability to get Marie to eat. Not much, but enough to sustain her. The tumor on her left side was now huge and they were afraid it would break through to the outside. It never did though.

It was obvious there were only a few days left in Marie's life. Her breathing was labored and you could hear a distinct rattle in her throat. Gene stayed close by her on the couch, or else he was beside her holding her in his arms. He had instructed everyone to notify him immediately if there was a change and he was not by her side at the moment it occurred. He was determined he would be with her in her last moments. Why not? They had been together daily for the past twenty-three years and he was determined to be there when she left this world. Gene had prayed so hard for Marie to live through Christmas Eve, Christmas Day and New Year's

Day. God answered those prayers. On New Year's Eve, Gene kissed Marie. She hardly responded but he knew she knew as she tried to return his kiss. On January 1st, Marie was completely unresponsive. Her medication had to be administered rectally or vaginally. All medication that was not absolutely necessary for pain control was dispensed with. Marie's breathing was more labored and the rattle in her throat was much worse. The rattle was coming from fluid build-up in the lungs and it was keeping the air from reaching the blood supply. What a horrible way to die. Gene knew death could come at any moment and as hard as he tried to prepare himself to act like a man, he knew when she went he would finally lose control.

On January 2nd, Marie went into a seizure. Gene was holding her in his arms. Everyone thought she was dying. Gene's emotions exploded and he begged God to take him also. Gene held her until the convulsions stopped and though she did not die, it was apparent she would not last long. Her breathing was growing more shallow while the laboring and the rattle worsened. That night a neighbor joined the death watch and they sat up all night. Around 4:00 A.M. on January 3rd, the neighbor went home and Gene lay down on the couch. He was awakened by Jean just after dawn and was told Marie's breathing pattern was worsening. Gene went to her side and sat on the small bath stool they were using by the sick bed for a chair. It was small and didn't occupy as much space as a chair would have. There he remained until the end came. At 7:45 A.M. Marie began rapid and shallow breathing. Her breaths were weak and trailing for a few minutes. She had hung on so long and suffered so severely. Gene knew she was hanging on for him, knowing what her loss would do to Gene. She tried so hard to live for him. God had other plans. At 7:50 A.M., Saturday, January 3, 1998, Marie turned her head slightly toward Gene, opened her eyes, tried to speak and took her last breath. Gene knew those words had to be "I love you." She was being held tightly in Gene's arms where she had been for the past several minutes. Just prior to death, Gene kissed her several times and told her, "It's all right, darling. You can let go. Go to God and I will follow as soon as I can." With those words, she seemed to relax and drift away. No more pain and suffering. She was now in the arms of her God. Rose Marie Hughes Sword, dead at the early age of fifty-one and taking with her the heart and love of Gene Sword for all eternity. Gene immediately called Eunice Jordan and calmly went back to Marie where he took her in his arms and held her until the natural warmth left her lifeless body. He now knew her soul had finally deserted its pain-racked and earthly home. It soared on heavenly wings to rest in the arms of her Lord. He had many tasks to attend to. The loss hit him in the face like an exploding bomb. He was totally numb and he acted in mechanical motions as if he were a robot. He called Hospice and the Hospice angel, Eunice Jordan, came as she said she would. He went back to her death bed and remained at her side until Eunice arrived. Eunice then took over and handled all of the legal and necessary notifications, along with the usual tasks that become necessary following a death. Then Marie left the home she had loved so much, for the last time. She had fought so long and hard to remain with Gene, but had lost the battle. Now Gene found himself standing alone in a cold and lonely place called "today." He had a strange devastating feeling of his inner self floundering helplessly in the nude, while all of humanity shamelessly stared. A helpless and horrible feeling, to be sure. He knew others had experienced it, but that was no help.

Gene's "Lady of the Morning," his "Lady Rose" now belonged to the eternal ages. A black and devouring grief had settled over him. He felt a hatred toward something he could not define. Then a whisper from deep within the recesses of his mind, shocked him back into reality and the world of reasoning. The whisper said, "Write for me." He immediately took a pad and pen and composed "The Good Ones First."

The Good Ones First

My Rose grew in a perfect garden
Fed by love and tender care
Kissed by rays of golden sunlight
There to grace the trellis bare

Then one day my Rose had vanished
My heart was left to mourn and thirst
My soul does marvel and does wonder
Why God takes "The Good Ones First."

He could not put the pen down. Flooding into his thoughts came words he had to record. He knew they were coming from her. The first night after her passing, he walked in the cold and drizzling rain. He stared into the dark overcast sky, but his eyes saw a starlit heaven. Gene searched in vain to see something special; a warning; some message. All the time the words kept forming in his mind. He went back into the silent house, where all were sleeping and feverishly labored over the mysterious words that kept pestering his consciousness. There was no doubt who was prodding him. Even in death, she was setting the pace for him to write. So he wrote.

I Hear a Whisper

I close my eyes and ponder
Where she now must be
Her wings must cleave a distant sky
Too far away to see

I call her name and wonder
If she hears the sound
My words are carried on the wind
As pulse in ears does pound

I stare into the cosmos
To see if I can see
Her image burned into my mind
Yet not a trace to be

If steps could only wander
Throughout the Milky Way
And if I called her loud enough
Perhaps she'd come and stay

Hush! . . . I hear a whisper!
It comes from far away
It is my love who speaks to me
She bids my soul to pray.

The day was dark and dreary when Marie journeyed to heaven. Within minutes of her death, a slow steady rain began to fall. The January day was unusually warm. Again, Gene had to write.

The Angels Cried

A cold rain falls this dreary day
Upon the earth so plain
That sleeps beneath winter's coat
Spring's hopes are dimmed again

It rained so hard the day she went
A horde of angels cried
Their healing tears washed the earth
To set our pain aside

For six long days their teardrops fell
The seventh sunlight came
Like God's creation story goes
They cried to ease our pain.

In the early nineties, the David Zeigler family had moved into the house next door to Gene and Marie. David was a minister. Soon the Zeigler family of four were the best of friends with Gene and Marie. Both Marie and Gene were very much impressed with David and his family. Marie wasn't much for going to organized church services, but she lived her religion from day to day. She was always ready to help anyone in need and to go the distance when necessary. She was extremely impressed with David's goodness and his willingness to stoop to help a child in need, as he did on many occasions. Marie told Gene, "When I die, I want David to conduct my funeral." Gene never forgot. Much to their disappointment, the Zeiglers moved away. They missed David, Sheila and their two children, Buba and Melissa. Gene never forgot Marie's request. They occasionally saw the Zeiglers after that and distance didn't dim the friendship.

When Marie and Gene knew that she was terminal and all hope was gone, Marie used Gene's legs and strong arms to lean on.

130

He was her messenger in organizing her pre-arranged funeral and carrying out her final wishes. One wish was to contact David Ziegler relative to conducting her funeral. David immediately accepted the task. He stated he needed a little notice but assured Gene he would be there. So it was. When Gene called him he came. In fact he, Sheila and Buba came for a prayer service just days before Marie passed away. She enjoyed it so very much, even through the horrible pain she was suffering. Once again, Gene summoned David and he came.

The funeral went very well. The chapel was packed and mourners were standing in the aisles. Marie had been very detailed about her funeral. She wanted David to officiate. She wanted her favorite poem, "Waste Not One Moment," and her favorite scripture passage read at the services. Her instructions were to place the scripture, poem and the small stuffed animals her friends had given her during her illness, in the casket with her. Gene saw to it that each "I" was dotted and that each "T" was crossed.

David officiated. Father Bob, a friend of Gene's, said a few words. Buffy Morgan read the poem. The local VFW honor guard and the Ladies' Auxiliary color guard conducted the military part of the services. Gene and Marie were both active in the local post and were attracted to becoming members by the good works the post did with children and old folks. Marie's second love was children. One of her last wishes was to have any money intended for flowers be donated to Covenant House, a home for wayward children. Marie's favorite hymns, "How Great Thou Art" and "Nearer My God to Thee," were performed as she requested.

David's sermon was an absolute masterpiece. It was easy to see why God had called him to the ministry. His remarks about Marie were extremely accurate. They were not falsely overflattering, as are heard in a lot of funerals. They were accurate but beautiful! Marie must have been well pleased.

Marie was interred at the National Cemetery in Houston, Texas, where one day Gene will rest with her. David, as usual, carried the ball all the way. He officiated at the grave-side services in spite of the pouring rain. Again his remarks were nothing short of miraculous and exhibited his propensity toward being a genius in handling people's emotions. Gene, for one, would be eternally grateful to this man. He found himself thinking, "If David or his family ever need me for anything at all and I am able to crawl, they shall have it."

The trip home was somber. Conversation was brief and sentences were terse. No one had eaten and it was late in the afternoon when the interment was completed. Gene knew Marie would want him to be as gracious as possible, even in his grief. He answered that challenge by taking the surviving family to dine at a large cafeteria on the way home. The food was good, but a somber air hung over the table. Much to Gene's surprise, he was able to eat, even if the food did sometimes stick in his throat. He did it more for show than for satisfying hunger. Inside he was dying a slow death emotionally but he vowed no one would see his tears.

One by one Marie's family went to their homes, until at last Gene was all alone, except for their faithful dog, Penny (a gift from David in years past). Gene spent hours weeping bitterly. There was no one to see his tears now and he could let go. At times he wondered if he was just a big baby. This man who had set such stock in being a real he-man. This macho machine, this adrenaline "junkie" of years past. But, then again, Gene had never known such love was possible, much less ever thought he would be fortunate enough to know it. He would never know it again and that was a hard cold fact. He knew he would never again look for a relationship. The loss of this one had been far too painful. He was well aware that he was so totally absorbed by his love for Marie, that he would probably be too blinded by that love to see it, if such an opportunity ever presented itself again. Then too, one never knows how intense a love will be until it is tested by time. Once the best is known, everything else is mundane.

What would he do with the rest of his life? At best, there

would not be a lot of life left, based on the history of longevity experienced by his family. How could he best use what time he had? His health wasn't anything to brag about, to be sure. It seemed one health problem followed another. The ugly thought of ending the pain himself crept in. It was easy. His pistol was on the night-stand beside him. Firing it wasn't anything new or difficult to him. All of a sudden he felt as if someone had slapped him full in the face. It was Marie again! He put that thought out of his mind. Again that strange whisper from far within himself bade him, "Write and pray." So write and pray he did. He went to church on Sunday; he prayed twice daily, sometimes more often and he wrote when possible. Then he knew what he must spend his time doing. She had loved his poetry so much, he decided he would write a book, dedicating the book and the poetry he created to her memory. But for now he had to live from day to day. He could write poetry because it comforted him to put his thoughts on paper, even if the comfort didn't last long. The book would have to wait for awhile. Gene would know when it was time to start the book. Besides, there were all those financial things he had to attend to.

The hospital bills were horribly high and insurance didn't cover all the expenses. Also, the insurance company was dragging its feet and the health providers were clamoring, as always, for their money now. Since the bills stacked up on his desk were over nine inches high, it would take a long time to audit them and get them paid. There were the life and annuity policies that had to be attended to. Marie's insurance license, credit card, driving license and identification cards had to be taken care of. He had to think about the bank accounts, retirement funds, not to mention the court records and court appearance for probate. There was more than enough to do for a couple of months.

Gene's children had to be notified. There were many former co-workers and acquaintances who had not been notified before because of time. Gene was far behind in all of his correspondence, his insurance business and his personal tasks. All of that had to be brought up to speed. He was happy he had so much to do. There were those damned bi-annual college hours of continuing education he had to complete before the last of April in order to keep his sales license up to date. That in itself would take quite a bit of time.

Gene worked at these tasks by day and he wrote by night. The writing helped with the loneliness. It was a little like talking to Marie. Although ashamed to admit it to his friends and family, he found himself talking to Marie at times. Just like she was in the room with him. He knew it was silly, but it helped. *But hold on there!* At times, it seemed he could hear a faint whisper that seemed to be Marie giving him answers. The whispers were far within his mind, like a tiny voice. Everyone experiences that strange inner whisper. It is probably the voice of conscience. Anyway, it was kind of nice to hear it as it was the only contact he had with Marie.

VIII

Dealing with Grief and Life after Loss

Gene started writing as if possessed by a demon. It was nothing for him to spend two days and nights at the computer, without stopping. Sheer exhaustion would put him down for twelve hours of sleep and back at the task again. It was as if he had only a limited amount of time in which to accomplish the book . . . and maybe he did. His pain was gargantuanous and only pen and paper offered any relief. Sometimes the pain was so great, the paper would be stained by tears when he finished. He longed to join Marie on one hand and on the other he longed to complete his writing task.

The following poems that were born as a result of that grief and mourning are now presented for the reader's perusal.

Near a Pine Tree

Beneath a pine tree by the road
My loved one sleeps in peace
In a field where others stay
Under fluffy clouds of fleece
One day too I there will lie
Until God calls us home
We then will fly on silver wings
To bow before His throne

Until that day when trumpets sound
To herald that glorious time
Back to the place where my love sleeps
I will go to the lonely pine
Upon the sod I there will kneel
And proclaim to her my love
While words I pray with aching heart
Will wing to Him above.

One More Time

I went again to where you sleep
It seems you're there no more
What is matter still remains
But what is spirit soars

With slumber comes the silence
When I stand upon the spot
I expect to hear you talking
But hurt when you do not

I will be glad when the marker's placed
And grass grows back in time
To cover scars caused by the grave
And my heart no more will pine.

The Highway

Life is but a superhighway
Spiraling on a spinning sphere
That is lost in endless cycles
Filled with love and filled with tears
From the day we start to journey
And wander down its crooked course
We'll taste the love and all the heartache
Battered by its ruthless force
We'll climb the hills and walk the valleys
Wade the streams and tread the snow
We'll talk of love and talk of sorrow
While dying some each mile we go
When the battle for us is over
And we finally stop to die
Let us hope the race was worth it
And that someone's left to cry.

Emptiness

When darkness chases the sun away
And the night takes over the land
Memories steal my heart away
As I reach to take her hand

No hand is there where I have reached
As I grip the empty air
I turn to stare at the place she sat
Only to find an empty chair

There stands the bed where once we lay
And dreamed our dreams of love
Now loneliness replaces her
Like mournful calling doves

How many days must come and go
Before my time is done?
Some day I'll be with her once more
To dwell in the land of the sun.

When My Mind Is Troubled

When my mind is troubled
And I know not where to turn
To find the peace and solitude
For which my heart does yearn

I steal away in silence
There to be alone
To pray to Him for comfort
Until He calls me home

My loved ones all have left me
To dwell with Him above
They reap rewards that He does give
While basking in His love

Here I remain in seas of strife
Beset by beast and man
I battle on in a wicked world
And long to take His hand.

Hear the Angels Sigh

Sometimes I walk alone at night
And stare into the sky
The stars and moon far overhead
Must hear the angels sigh

At times when I in awe do watch
I wonder right out loud
If I in time again will see
Her face there in a cloud

Will I ever see her shining smile
Beaming down at me?
Or must I stare at empty space
Until at last I'm free?

I know we'll meet again one day
For He has promised me
Because our "love light" burned so bright
"Together" we shall be.

Vale of Tears

I stare into the mirror glass
At age lines on my face
I feel the weight of loneliness
And I yearn to take her place

The sadness of her passing
Cut holes inside of me
That tore my life asunder
And caused my heart to flee

I walk the road of lonely men
Too numb to feel the love
That faithful friends try to show
To me from her above

Someday, I hope to find my way
Into the stream of life
For now I tread in vales of tears
Awash in seas of strife

Confound the curse that brought me here!
To flounder on the sands
Which dooms my soul to loveless days
And wander barren lands.

In the Arms of Marie

Once more the stars are calling
While the wind is dancing free
And my thoughts are ever turning
To the love of "My Marie"

If I should search forever
I know I would not find
A better friend or lover
Or a heart that is as kind

When the autumn leaves are falling
And winter's breath chills the land
I'll walk along the meadow
While she seems to take my hand

So I'll recall with fondness
All the love she had for me
And the happy hours of gladness
In the arms of "My Marie."

Twilight Falling

Beautiful shades of night are falling
As twilight steals the day
Gentle waves are gaily lapping
At the beach in the bay

Nighttime skies are growing darker
A trillion stars come out to play
As silver moonbeams earthward falling
Turning nighttime into day

I sit alone on my verandah
Watching fireflies start to fly
While thoughts of her are cascading
And burning teardrops sting my eyes

How we loved to sit at twilight
Watching shadows growing long
I'd hold her hand and steal a kiss
While the night birds sang their song.

The Memory of Marie

The feel of her tender touch
The twinkle in her eye
The tinkling bells when she spoke
The sunshine in her smile

I long to walk with her once more
Through endless fields of flowers
Along the banks of babbling brooks
In the mist of springtime showers

But alas! This will not be
My memory must suffice
Sustaining love that my heart feels
For the lady that was my wife

The golden gift that we call health
Forsakes her far too soon
Now I'm alone to face each day
With the calling of the loon.

The Order of Things

Fresh is springtime in the morning
Like the day that follows birth
Like the first day of creation
Like the making of the earth

From the soul springs hope eternal
An enigma not understood
Nonetheless it gives a meaning
To our lives as well it should

These are truths we must consider
When one we love is called away
It helps explain the choice of going
And gives a reason why we must stay.

Memories

I quietly lay beside her
While she was deep in sleep
The warmth of her nearness
Nearly made me weep

The sweetness of her presence
Made my heart fare well
The magnitude of her love
No human tongue can tell

She sang my praise in public
And tended every need
While asking naught for herself
She sowed "the lover's seed"

The fondness of her memory
Now graces thought and deed
Engulfing every moment
That sets my soul to bleed

No one on earth replaces
All she meant to me
I struggle through endless days
And cling to memories

No one sees the tears I cry
Or knows the pains that be
In silence moving day to day
While sailing lonely seas.

Green Was the Valley

How green was the valley
Where I strolled with you
Through meadows filled with blossoms
Thirsting for the dew

How sweet was the fragrance
That wafted on the breeze
Along the course of babbling brook
Tempting wayward bees

Your smile was like the labor
Of some skillful artist's brush
On canvas drenched in sunshine
'Neath hills of virgin lush

How precious are the memories
Of moments spent with you
We frolicked in the sunlight
Beneath the sky so blue

These memories are my mementos
I have locked inside my heart
As long as I recall them
Never shall we part.

The Voice of Love

The voice of love is calling
Across a vast expanse of time
To this mortal heart yet yearning
As it flounders weak and blind
In a wasteland stark and lonely
Where storms and tempest blow
While it hopes to journey "yonder"
On a ship that sails too slow

How impatient is the longing
To know that love once more
How painful is the yearning
To walk upon that shore
How intense is the memory
Of the love that's gone away
How happy is the prospect
Of her love again one day.

Dreams

Sleep finally comes
When thoughts of the day
That troubled my mind
Have faded away

Then blankets of dreams
Spread over me
Like the arms of a love
That sets my soul free

She beckons to me
From stars to the west
There out of my dreams
With hands that I've pressed

My mind dimly sees
There in the mist
Calling to me
Are lips that I've kissed

I hear the voice of my love
Calling far away
I miss the tender moments
That are gone by light of day.

Empty Arms and Heartaches

Empty arms and heartaches
Greet me each new day
With loneliness and solitude
Since you went away

Raindrops and storm clouds
Are present where I stay
Sad songs and poetry
Never go away

Teardrops stain the pillow
Where I sleep each night
If I could only change things
I try with all my might

I know we'll meet again someday
Then I these words can say
"Empty arms and heartaches
Now have passed away."

Winds of Winter

The north wind sings a sad song
And takes a bitter bite
It roars about my empty home
And steals the peace and quiet

The sky is gray and overcast
Not a single star in sight
Ominous gloom is all about
And I miss her so tonight

She left my side a month ago
My sleep she steals at night
By memories I can't forget
Though I try with all my might

Perhaps the spring will change the mood
When life once more will flow
Into the earth where now she dwells
And banish winter's snow.

You Cannot Hold a Snowflake

You cannot catch a snowflake
Concealed inside your hand
Or hold onto a wisp of smoke
That drifts across the land
You cannot gather dewdrops
That fall upon the grass
And there reflect the rays of light
Like shards of broken glass

These enigmatic phantoms
All seem to come and go
Like sounds of elfin angels
We cannot hear but know
They're like the realm of fleeting love
We hold dear to our hearts
But feel the cutting, searing pain
When that love departs.

The Piper's Song

Many dawns come to find me
At a window with my face against the glass
My nights are filled with pacing
And my mind so tortured by the past

I stare at dewdrops shining
Like a million flawless diamonds on the grass
I know that loneliness is with me
And from my lips this cup will never pass

The morning's filled with singing
By the songs of a thousand little birds
My heart should soar with gladness
But it's like my ears have never heard

I reach to draw the curtains
To try and block the world outside at last
But shattered dreams are there to haunt me
That cut my soul like jagged broken glass

I feel so cold and naked
While I tremble in the night so dark and long
While I ponder the equation
Of how to pay the piper for his song.

Carpet of Dreams

Dreams my magic carpet
Take me back to spring once more
When we were young and so in love
In those heady days of yore

She was young while I was older
And she believed the words I said
I gave my heart and soul to her
With the poems that I read

We laughed and often frolicked
Upon meadows green with grass
In the silence of the evening
When I listen I hear her laugh

It's just an echo of a memory
Fragmented by the wind of time
That disappears in the distance
And leaves a tortured mind behind.

Card Games

There were friends and zesty card games
Those friends came to serve us well
And, oh, how we loved those friends!
The poet's pen can never tell

Judy's heart was truly fiery
She was a classy little lass
Charles was quiet and all laid back
He never gave any "sass"

Marie was smooth and oh so cunning
She had a trick up every sleeve
While Gene was known to "blow his stack"
Sometimes the cards he would relieve

We whiled away those happy hours
With the friends we all loved so
But now there're only three friends left
And oh, My God! We miss her so!

Good-bye Marie!

Journey of Sentiment

I spent the night with Charles and Judy
I felt the warmth inside their home
They are friends we often stayed with
And with that thought I felt alone

When we sat beside their table
I chanced to stare at the empty mat
My heart then broke into many pieces
The place was where Marie once sat

I tried hard to choke back feelings
And not to show how I felt
But Judy knew how I was hurting
I thought for sure my heart would melt

I love those friends there's no denying
But to visit now hurts you see
Each time I go I feel her presence
Which speaks of times spent with Marie

But I must take the love they offer
And our trio just let it be
While we recall the days back yonder
In those golden times of revelry.

Back to the First Home

Today I went into the city
To the street we knew so well
I stood upon the walk and pondered
Trying not to ring the bell

It was our first home when we married
Rich in happy gone-by days
I seemed to hear her sweet voice echo
Inside the alcoves and the bays

Gone are roses that she loved so
Camellias, jasmine, and flax of blue
And because of inattention
I knew they went their way like you

I never cease to be amazed now
At all the places that she can be
It seems she's present in all creation
In all creation except with me.

There Will Never Be Another

I got over Frankie Atwell
Christina Miller and Pauline Wong
I had it hard with Irma Richards
She hurt me some but not for long

There's only one girl I can remember
That made me tremble deep down inside
I'd give them all for a single moment
Spent with "My Rose" before she died

There has never been another
Who made me weak when at my side
Or that gave me the love I needed
As Marie did when she tried

Things get bad for me in summer
When the night grows damp and long
It gets worse for me come winter
When they play those lonesome songs

Please don't ask me for I won't tell you
And you can bet your sweet life I lied
Because there's never been one better
Than Marie was when she tried.

I Find Teardrops on My Pillow

Your clothes in your closet
Remind me of you
They change my thoughts to sadness
And my mood into blue

Your lipsticks on the dresser
In many shades of red
They rob my heart of gladness
Inflicting painful wounds of dread

I pick up your perfume bottle
And hold it in my hand
I smell the fragrant odor
As teardrops start again

When I wake up each morning
Before my daily chores I start
I find teardrops on my pillow
And searing pain within my heart.

The Redbud Tree

Her redbud tree is blooming
It heralds the coming of the spring
This fact is made more evident
By the many birds that flit and wing

They perch among its branches
And sing a host of different songs
This year things all seem different
Because the days are hard and long

She watched for its annual blooming
Every spring that came our way
She knew the redbud's blossoms
Meant spring had come to stay

She walked, watched, and pondered
The beauty of its bloom
But life is often fickle
Her time was cut too short too soon

The redbud tree is dying
There is nothing that I can do
I doubt this blooming beauty
Will ever see another dew.

Marie's Giant White Oak Tree

The stately giant white oak tree
That grows beside our home
With its roots firmly planted
In sandy clay and loam
Has provided shade and comfort
To me and "My Marie"
And we grew to love it greatly
This giant white oak tree

We loved it green in summer
The brilliant colors in the fall
We loved to sit beneath its shade
While mockingbirds did call
I still love that old oak tree
But not that much today
For my heart is filled with sadness
"My Marie" has gone away.

Pretty Little Bird Songs

The mockingbird and titmouse
Singing on the hill
Awoke us in the morning
With songs both sweet and shrill

Through many hours we listened
Lying close and very still
As if we both were afraid
This magic cup would spill

Too soon the spell was broken
The songbirds flew away
And took those happy moments
From then until this day

Many birds have come to ply
Their songs upon the hill
Now that I am all alone
Their songs no longer thrill.

Tomorrow Never Comes

When the long and lonely shadows
Bring the end to the day
And the sun that warmed the earth
In the sky no longer stays
Cold and morbid feelings
Seem to reach and grip the heart
And rob the mind of solace
When the nighttime finally starts

Yesterdays are gone forever
And tomorrow never comes
Today is all that ever will be
And our race is never run
We simply stare across horizons
And dream of days full of fun
We battle "Demon Lonely"
As we go from sun to sun.

Wedding Ring

A golden diamond wedding ring
Graced her finger bold
Its brilliance glimmered like the sun
In satin motif old

She proudly showed her left hand off
Wherever she would go
It wasn't pride in worldly things
That caused her to act so

She wanted all the world to know
And everyone to see
The ring was just a symbol
Of the love she felt for me

Now my days I spend alone
And of the past reflect
Our rings now hang from golden chain
I wear around my neck

They remind me of the one I love
And the love she had for me
Just like her I'll wear these rings
For all the world to see.

The Land That Knows No Sorrow

Do not weep for me, my friends,
Or burden your hearts with sorrow
I've simply gone to wait for you
To join you come tomorrow

One day you'll shed these earthly bonds
When your spirit is free to borrow
All the dreams your hearts can hold
In the land that knows no sorrow

When you journey to the shore
Of golden silver sand
I'll be there to greet you friend
And to take you by the hand

Until the day we meet again
Remember me with gladness
And all the time you spent with me
Without the cloak of sadness

If anyone who knows these words
Has ever harmed my name
Before my God I now forgive
And I pray you do the same.

In our God's name, fare well and prosper!

It was late March of 1998 and Gene had to complete thirty clock hours of continuing education in the insurance field to maintain his license. This had to be done before his license expired in late April. He had already completed fifteen such hours and had registered for the remaining requirement for the 26th and 27th of March. He felt his heart skip a beat and jump into his throat when he realized that the last day fell on Marie's birthday! He just had to put flowers on her grave that day and again on the 29th, as the 29th was their anniversary. He would stay with Judy and Charlie both to visit with them again and because they lived so close to the school he would attend.

The class was finally over and he rushed to the cemetery before the office closed. The lady attendant was very helpful. She gave him the rules for placing flowers on graves, told him where the required flower containers were and where the nearest florist shop was located. He thanked her and made his way to the florist shop. There he purchased roses. When he returned to the cemetery he placed the flowers in the container and then placed the container on Marie's grave. They looked so good and proper there, blowing in the stiff breeze that was sweeping across the vast expanse of the national cemetery. The ground keepers had done a wonderful job. The site was freshly sodded and well kept. Gene knew the summer would cause the grass to fill in around the grave and make it a green, plush resting place for "His Lady." That was exactly why he had chosen this cemetery as Marie's final resting place, for the perpetual maintenance.

For a long time Gene stood by her grave alone. Tears streamed down his face as he wished "His Lady" a happy birthday. He told her all the news and especially about "her book" that was almost finished. Gene didn't forget Marie's baby (Penny, their dog) and that she sent her love. He told her about his children who were visiting him almost weekly now. She surely must have been glad. Gene couldn't help but wonder: if someone came along would they think he was crazy, talking to a grave? Somehow, he didn't care. He loved her and this was therapeutic to him. He would be back again and again.

What in God's name would he do with the rest of his life? At this point he did not know. Gene knew life would go on, good or bad, and carry him along with it. Only time would answer that fateful question.

Looking Over My Shoulder

Looking over my shoulder
At a life left behind
I see the love that is gone now
And it tortures my mind
Her smiling expression
Is staring at me
And I know that forever
My heart won't be free

For ours was a real love
Like the stars love the sea
And it's plain that forever
Such another won't be

Looking over my shoulder
At a time we once knew
And all the nostalgia
Forever making me blue
One day I will journey
To the place where you are
And we'll dwell there together
Among billions of stars

For ours was a real love
Like the stars love the sea
And it's plain that forever
Such another won't be.

I See in the Stars

I see in the stars
Among their profusion
A love that is gone
To the Cosmos to dwell
And there to await
The joining of our souls
When my turn will come
To ride on time's swell

I can not despair
In the depths of the lonely
For she has decreed
That life is to live

So I look to the stars
When I long for her presence
To fill the void
That I feel in my heart
And there I see
Among their profusion
Her countenance once more
And she'll never depart

I can not despair
In the depths of the lonely
For she has decreed
That life is to live.

A Place for Me

Shadows creep across my garden
Where roses bloom and grow
Nostalgia fills my heart with feelings
As I ponder why she had to go

Her passing left a cavern
That nothing will ever fill
I go through boring mundane motions
While sadness daily builds

I am staring through a morbid tunnel
At the end no light I see
Her light that lit my way is gone now
That light no more on earth will be

Her light is shining up in heaven
Where angels now sing with glee
She tells the Master of my coming
And they prepare a place for me

I long to hear the trumpets blaring
And to cross that tranquil sea
I believe with all my heart
She has prepared a place for me.

Hallowed Ground

Across a field that is green with grass
And markers that lay in neat rows
There is a spot of sacred ground
Where my troubled heart often goes

Beyond the trees stands the tower
Where mournful bells often ring
There are two flagpoles that touch the sky
And the flags that fly are serene

Beautiful flowers now mark the spot
Where forever my love lies in sleep
My heart often goes to visit her there
Beneath the still earth cold and deep

One day I too will lay here with her
Where we'll rest through all of time
Till the day that we both rise up again
When love is no longer so blind.

Thank You!

Thank you, for the times you stood beside me
When sorrow seemed to tear my heart apart.
Thank you, for your gentle touch of kindness
When my sunshine left and made the day so dark.
Thank you, for the comfort of your presence
When time seemed to drag my spirits down.
Thank you, for being you in all your splendor
I'm so glad to know that you are still around.
Thank you, for the loving way you generate
A secret tender spot inside my heart.
Thank you, for the peace when you are present
That I feel each time we meet until we part.

Loving You Was Easy

You hear me weep beside the stone
That marks the place where you now stay
I softly tread the sod above you
And try in vain to face each day.

You know the pain that dwells within
This heart inside my chest
And all the lonely hours I spend
Recalling times that we loved best.

Oh, how I long to hear your voice
And to feel your hand in mine
I yearn so much to taste your lips
And to ease my tortured mind.

Loving you for me came easy
As I marked each place in time
I'd gladly trade all my tomorrows
To hold your body next to mine.

For now the tolling bells of time
Must ring out for me alone
But I'm taking little comfort
From their mellow ringing tone.

An Angel Fell

Once a band of angels
Flew too close to the ground
One of them chanced to fall
And she's the one I found

I nursed her broken wings
And soothed her shattered heart
She chose to stay around awhile
But I knew, someday we'd part

A man and an angel
Can not abide for long
One day she flew away again
And took from me my song

The bitter fruit of anguish
Is my companion every day
Though I'm thankful for the time we had
I knew an angel couldn't stay

I peer around the corners
Of what is left of my life
Never holding onto anything
But her leaving brings me strife.

I would like to end this book with a very terse and perhaps somewhat unusual poem. It has a lot of meaning for me and I hope it is of benefit to you also. It is called "Poets Cry."

Poets Cry

Lovers swoon
Singers croon
Millers grind
Jewelers wind
Poets cry
Heroes die
Sometimes poets
Are heroes

Drivers drive
Divers dive
Walkers walk
Talkers talk
Poets cry
Heroes die
Sometimes poets
Are heroes.